Mr & Mrs Kota,
Please enjoy.

TENACIOUS

THE CONFUCIAN CAPITALISM OF CHINA,
THE TENACITY OF THE AMERICAN CHARACTER,
AND THE NEXT ECONOMIC RENAISSANCE.

Wealth Shift Publishing

Copyright © 2011, Wealth Shift Publishing

ISBN: 978-0-9852762-0-1 (Soft cover)
          978-0-9852762-1-8 (Hard cover)

Library of Congress Control Number: 2011943835

All Rights Reserved. No part of this book may be reproduced or transmitted in any form or by any means, electronic or mechanical, including photocopying, recording, or by any information storage and retrieval system without written permission from the author, except for the inclusion of brief quotations in a review.

Printed in the United States of America.

Author photo: Mallary Baskerville

Table of Contents

Introduction vii
    GDP, Meet DNA   viii
    There Is No Them   ix
    Tenacious Means Tough   x

Chapter 1: The Society Inside Us 1
    Now Entering DNA Accumulation Zone   2
    Character and Dominance   3
    Derailing s-DNA   5
    What About War?   6
    Genocides: s-DNA Erased and Inflamed   7
    Military Occupation: Societies Held in Isolation   8
    Emigration and Immigration: Societies' Pushes
        and Pulls   10
    Immigration Overwhelming   11
    Emigration and the End of the Renaissance   12
    The Incredible Shrinking Ireland   13

Chapter 2: Immigration in America:
How They Became Us 16
    Europe: Modern and Mean   17
    America Transformed, in Two Massive Waves   19
    The America They Built, the Americans We Became   20
    The Raw Material of American s-DNA   21

The Contemporary Expression of American s-DNA	22
Immigrants Pushed the Frontier West	24
Immigrants Were the Muscle of America's New Industries	24
Immigrants Were the Owners of American Small Business	26
Immigrants Helped America Endure Its Greatest Trial	26
Emigrants Allowed Europe to Deepen What Makes Them European	27
We Are All This and More	28

Chapter 3: China Now: Communal and Conflicted 29

How Confucius Created China	31
Confucianism Under Communism: Violently Agreeing	33
A Few Words on Shame	35
Contemporary Contradictions: It's How They Roll	37

Chapter 4: Mommy and Her Chinese Teenager 39

Getting All Wobbly on Two Wheels	42
Bump One: A Massively Overheated Real Estate Market	43
Bump Two: The Limits of Steroid Stimulus	45
Bump Three: Kids Today	48
Bump Four: Little Emperors and Their Smooth, Soft Hands	49
Bump Five: The Rise of Middle-Class Militants and the Fall of Single-Party Politics	50

Table of Contents

    Bump Six: Social Unrest, Meet Social Malaise   52
    Bump Seven: Widespread Environmental Degradation and Overwhelmed Public Health   53
    Bump Eight: Let Them Eat Coal   54
  The Long Road of Nations   55

Chapter 5: Tenacity in the Tank: The U.S. Then, Now, and in the Future 57
  The Civil War   58
  Trust-Busting and the Panic of 1907   61
  The Crash of 1929 and the Great Depression   63
  The American Secret Sauce   67

Chapter 6: Innovators, Imitators, and Immigrants: Challenging Assumptions 69
  Belief: America Doesn't Make Anything Anymore   70
  Belief: Only Manufacturing Economies Are Successful Economies   72
  Belief: China Is Beating Us in Our Own Game of Innovation   75
  Belief: China Is Out-Educating the U.S., and Doing a Better Job Preparing Its Young People to Lead the Global Economy   78
  Belief: The Chinese Economy Is Expanding So Quickly, It's Just a Matter of Time Before They Overtake the U.S.   82
  Belief: Demographics Are Working Against the U.S.   84

**Chapter 7: Riding the Continuums: This Way
to an American Renaissance** 86

Maslow Meets s-DNA	87
Tenacity 3.0	89
Fundamentals for a New Century	91
But...but...but...	92
"Recalculating"	93
Pink Slips and Green Cards	94
And Then, There's China	97
Scenario 1: China Falters	98
Scenario 2: The U.S. Contracts	99
Stay Tenacious: Seven Ideas to Fight For	99
The Opportunistic American	99
We're Getting Older...Then, Younger than Everyone Else	100
Dollars Rule, Now and in the Future	102
Immigration Refreshes Innovative Capacity	102
When in Doubt, Think Higher Tech	103
Emerging Markets Are Immature Markets	103
People Don't Change	104
A Final Thought	104

About the Author 106

Acknowledgments 107

Introduction

Where are you from?

We ask it when we meet someone new. We ask—with curiosity and kindness, one hopes—when we detect an accent of a different region or a different country. We ask it, and it's asked of us: Where are you from?

In previous generations, the question was heavy with importance. Meeting a stranger meant encountering *otherness*. There was mystery, and fear. Today the shifting demographic tides of our modern world, the relative ease of global travel, and the border neutrality of the Internet have all dialed down the mystery. Fear, however, seems to be making a comeback, especially in the United States.

The long-simmering resentment of Hispanics has heated up, especially when there are political points to be scored. And now there's a new fear spreading across the land of the free—or rather, the same fear with a different and more mysterious face: China.

The steep ascent of the Chinese economy, along with comparatively slow economic growth in the U.S., has many Americans feeling uneasy. Business leaders, elected officials, investors, educators, and a lot of intelligent regular folks are looking fearfully at the Middle Kingdom. Instead of seeing a complex and conflicted nation struggling to jump from the seventeenth century to the twenty-first, they see a monolithic economic juggernaut devouring scarce resources, American jobs, and American prestige.

Oh boy, here comes another one.

Since the post-WWII boom quieted in the 1970s, prognosticators have claimed that someone other than the U.S. has the new economic mojo. In the early 2000s, a unified Europe and their single currency was portrayed as the economy to fear, if not emulate. Same with Japan a decade or so earlier. That didn't happen, nor should it have. There were rampant fears that Mexico was going to drain the vitality from the U.S. manufacturing sector while India skimmed the cream from high tech. Wrong again.

All these nations are populated with smart, hardworking people. If you were seated next to one on a flight and struck up a "what's your business" conversation, you'd likely learn something interesting and even useful. And sooner or later, you'd get around to the question you probably wanted to ask all along: Where are you from?

But if you really want to understand how a nation's economy can thrive—if you want a more penetrating view of where to invest—the best question to ask is not "Where are you from?"

It's "*Who* are you from?"

GDP, MEET DNA

Today even non-scientists have a reasonably accurate understanding of DNA and the role it plays in shaping our individual biology. DNA carries your genes, and genes are the blueprints you begin with to build the house called you. The blueprints don't tell you what color to paint the trim, but they do clearly specify the architectural style. For better or worse, you're stuck in the house designed by your genes. So are your kids and even their kids' kids.

So, genes create individuals and individuals create societies. This is a book about societies and the economies they develop.

In my first book, *Wealth Shift*, I defined the multiple ways in which one group of American individuals, the aging Baby Boomers, were going to play an oversized role in the U.S. and even the global economy. I asked readers to look underneath economic data and policy decisions to see the demographic forces shaping them. *Wealth*

Shift debuted in 2003 and much of what those pages anticipated has happened, or is happening now.

I return to *Wealth Shift* not to congratulate myself, but to illustrate to the readers of *Tenacious* that my focus has always been on the macro rather than the micro. In *Wealth Shift* the focus was demographics. In *Tenacious*, I'm digging further to expose a deep vein of national character and shared values that I call societal DNA. My goal is to help you make better decisions on *where* to invest your attention and your wealth (the micro) by understanding the societal DNA of *who* you're investing in (the macro). Remember the question isn't "where," it's "who."

THERE IS NO THEM

I believe in the United States. That's not political or sentimental. I don't have a flag in my front yard or Norman Rockwell on my office walls. My belief is rooted in my own study of American economic history and first-hand experiences with individuals and industries tapping into this history to forge promising futures.

In the pages ahead I'll argue hard for the U.S., but I'm not interested in creating enemies.

China gets a lot of ink here, and if you restrict your view to the current news cycle, it's easy to imagine the U.S. and China as economic adversaries. They are competitors, of course, but also partners in helping to strengthen the American economy by lifting the living standards of millions of Chinese citizens. I'm going to take you into the foundational structures of Chinese societal DNA. These are remarkable people who deserve our respect and admiration.

The Chinese people are also expressing something essential and immutable in how they manage the economic Frankenstein they've brought to life. It's a monster that no one should want to fall down.

TENACIOUS MEANS TOUGH

Tenacious takes its title from the societal DNA of the U.S. This deep vein in the American character is layered with the fierce striving of immigrants, initially Europeans and then Asians and Hispanics. The individuals who set out for the New World brought with them traits and values that had no place in sixteenth-, seventeenth-, eighteenth-, or nineteenth-century Europe.

They wanted opportunity, not hierarchy. Ownership, not serfdom. Ideas and invention, not crowns and courtly rituals. Leaving was hard, the journey was treacherous, and the new beginnings were heartbreakingly difficult. Setting aside the scourge of slavery for a moment, no one came to America by accident. They fought to get here and then fought to survive—including the freed African slaves. They were tenacious. And they are us.

One

The Society Inside Us

People around here are about the same.

What might sound like an offhand assessment of a bland small town is actually a deceptively powerful macroeconomic truth. To tap into it, you'll need a view that's much wider than the people in your town, small or large.

True, the difference in appearance and behavior between any two individuals, or any 200 or 2,000, can be vast. Individuals have singular personalities and possess truly unique gifts. They are snowflakes, as the saying goes, and unlike any other snowflake in the vast history of frozen precipitation.

But here's the thing about all those different snowflakes: They're still snowflakes.

They're not different from each other in the way apples, oranges, and bulldozers are. With snowflakes, the difference between this one and that one is evident only when you examine the individual crystalline structures very closely. Snowflake anatomy, if you will, and this isn't an anatomy book.

In these pages, I'm asking you to ignore individual flakes and stay focused on the accumulated snowfall...to imagine the weight of generations, falling year after year after year...to see the landscapes that are gradually built up by all these very similar snowflakes, and to think critically about what makes those landscapes different from each other.

Holding that mindset is not always going to be easy, especially for American readers who are infused with that particularly American brand of individuality. What's more, we've all been exposed to diversity messages meant to alternately celebrate the differences between us or minimize them to the tune of an inane, politically correct Disney song.

It's actually not a small world after all. It's a big and complex human ecosystem, but it can be understood in large chunks of population—big piles of snow that take the shape of individual nations. And yes, this is dangerous territory.

Anytime someone starts making broad generalizations about people, especially people "over there," the dreaded s-word is whipped out: stereotypes. Understood. I acknowledge the peril and invite you to hold judgment until I've made my arguments with something more robust than labels: data and logic.

NOW ENTERING DNA ACCUMULATION ZONE

The scientists at the Human Genome Project deserve a lot of credit. When they set out to map the human DNA in 1990, they expected to be hunched over their microscopes (and monitors) until 2005—fifteen long years. Thanks to advances in computing science and a lot of international cooperation, they presented a "rough draft" in 2000, five years ahead of schedule. Since then, they've refined the sequence down to individual chromosomes, and learned a lot about how this baseline structure affects the humans wrapped around it.

For one, there are a lot fewer genes than they anticipated. Most predictions said that humans had up to 100,000 genes. But the Human Genome Project has lowered that number to as few as 20,000. And here's the one that got my attention: In 2002, the International HapMap Project started charting genetic codes among various ethnic groups and concluded that from person to person, across the planet, humans differ from one another by about 0.1 percent.

So, genetically speaking, there's one tenth of a percentage point separating you and any other human on Earth. And if our genes define our origins so similarly, can the same be said of our actions? Is there a behavioral parallel to the fixed imprint of our genes? I believe so; it's our character.

Character arrives with an interesting set of meanings. It's a measure of both a person's integrity and his eccentricity. It's a role people play, and a symbol in a larger system. Each has relevance as I build the foundation of this book's thesis. Character is the combination of qualities that *distinguish* people, or groups, from each other. It's what makes them different. But I hold that character is not so distinguishing once a lot of characters are in view.

Once characters become a group, especially a nation, individual character synthesizes and blends into a *national* character. National character is not a precise enlargement of any single individual, yet it does represent what's most common among the mass of individual characters. What's more, national character is not merely a scorecard of the most *common* traits; it's what a nation *values* most. And, for economists and investors, that's where things start to get really interesting.

CHARACTER AND DOMINANCE

Let's start with a short science lesson on how traits are inherited from the previous generation, i.e., Mom and Dad. It's an everyday observation that children tend to resemble their parents, but it is equally obvious that the resemblance is not exact. Tall parents do not always produce tall children; children with red hair do not necessarily have redheaded parents. The reason is genes, and each gene influences our traits in one of three ways: dominant, co-dominant, or recessive. When a dominant gene meets a recessive gene, the dominant trait will emerge. But we all have a mixture of each kind. For example, if you have brown hair you may still carry the recessive gene for blond hair—it just got overruled by another brown hair gene that your other parent brought to the party. It takes two recessive genes for a recessive trait, like blond hair or blue eyes, to emerge. Skin color, on the other hand, is a co-dominant trait, and when those genes combine they simply mix. That's why bi-racial individuals typically have a skin color somewhere between that of their parents.

Okay, that's Genetics 101, minus about a hundred, but it's enough for our purposes because aspects of dominant and recessive genes have a place in our exploration of national character, too. In other words, there's a national equivalent to brown hair. Let's start with a generic example: a cultural tendency to strong family orientation.

It's no accident of demographics when there's a clear and measurable family-first orientation in a population of people. That orientation deepens over generations as the society evolves. As a people, they construct the norms that their society values and those norms are large-scale reflections of what they value individually. As a society, they reward the individuals who most visibly embody those values. Exemplars emerge, and are lionized. The Family Man or Family Woman becomes an icon, and the opposites become pariahs. Both the good and the bad examples become extremely potent symbols. "Be like him, not like that loser." The Family Man or Woman becomes what moms and dads want their kids to become; it's who they reward with praise and who they chose to lead them. The public imagination has a well-defined ideal, and family orientation becomes the dominant gene in the society.

These norms can be visible, especially to viewers with some objective distance, but how they are transmitted is largely invisible. They are habits of mind, and a kind of institutional currency

The Society Inside Us

that flows from the stories we hear sitting on a grandparent's lap to the shared moments in the public square. Within each moment are codes of conduct and social obligations—they are external expressions, but they emanate from deep internal structures. And they have economic relevance.

Economist Adam Smith has been rightly lionized as the father of modern economics and capitalism. In his widely-cited *The Wealth of Nations*, he describes optimal economic activity as "the invisible hand of the market." But before *The Wealth of Nations*, Smith wrote *The Theory of Moral Sentiments*. In this lesser-known work, he described how social interactions and the unconscious desire for esteem shapes individual behavior and drives micro-economic activity. In fact, Smith was insistent that the hard-headed concepts in *Wealth of Nations* rest on the foundation of moral sentiments. But today, the *Wealth of Nations* has become a *de facto* policy guide in capitalist societies, and *Moral Sentiments* is rarely discussed. Maybe it's time to rebalance Adam Smith.

Admittedly, character is not biological on an individual level, and human behavior is a jumble of influences, but on the scale of societies it's difficult to image anything with the same enduring potency and reinforcing affect as these deep cultural values. They become societal DNA, and we'll return to this idea throughout the rest of the book. Societal DNA will show up so often, let's shorten it now: s-DNA.

Every country has a distinct s-DNA deep in the national boiler, and once their train starts moving in one direction, it's simply not going to veer too far off that track—that's an intuitive notion to most readers. So let's see if there's some new territory to explore.

DERAILING S-DNA

S-DNA accumulates slowly. It's expressed as governments, educational systems, art, even religions. For the sake of argument, think of s-DNA as society itself. Now, when was the last time you saw a society making a real and sustained change? Not something on the surface like a new political direction or a technological advance. True, those may dramatically change individual lives and may, in fact, change *your* life, but we're not looking at individuals. Consider the question at the level of population, and think about when you've observed a society making a real and sustained change.

It's sort of a trick question. Societies are like objects moving in space: They will never stop unless acted upon by outside forces. Gravity and friction combine to change the course of a moving object, often quite abruptly. Societies can also change abruptly, relatively speaking, when they encounter one or more of four external forces: emigration, immigration, military occupation, or genocide.

WHAT ABOUT WAR?

It's tempting to overstate the societal impact wars can have. Yes, they are violent upheavals from the norm (especially when they happen in a society's back yard) and historians do some of their best work when conflict and war are driving the text. We remember wars longer than we remember treaties, but they don't usually derail the society that suffers the most impact. The wholesale slaughter of WWI wasn't enough to fundamentally change British, French, German, Greek, Turkish, or Russian societies. We learned how to kill each other on an industrial scale, and the seeds of WWII were planted in those bloody trenches, but the natures of the societies involved moved about as far as the lines on the post-war map—not far, if at all. Japan endured the worst weapons that war has yet to produce, and yet after the war their society continued in much the same way as it had for hundreds, if not thousands of years. Japan was defeated; Japanese society was not.

Genocide and prolonged military occupations have a greater impact on societies and s-DNA than the actual fighting of war. And to our infamy as civilized people, the examples could continue for pages.

GENOCIDES: S-DNA ERASED AND INFLAMED

The historical records fail to capture the full measure of genocide. Genocide took place before the written word, and does still in our lifetimes. Millions of non-combatants have been killed in Rwanda, Darfur, and the former Yugoslavia. The fate of those societies and the trajectories of their respective s-DNA will be recorded by others. From this moment in history, we can see the generational impacts of only those genocides that occurred many decades, if not centuries, in the past.

In the late 1800s, Russian soldiers killed an estimated 400,000 Caucasians, or 90 percent of the population. Today, we'll find what's left of their s-DNA in the fierce fighters of Chechnya.

No one knows for sure what the populations of North and South America were before the European colonization began. Some say as many as 100 million Native Americans on both continents were killed, decimating entire societies and essentially erasing their s-DNA from human history. In Australia, the Aborigines endured a similar fate.

In the Holocaust, six million Jews perished. I'll leave it to Jewish historians and sociologists to diagnose the full injury to their s-DNA, but here's my view: the Jews who now inhabit Israel carry an s-DNA that has been hardened by trauma. When Jews repeat "never again," it is both a source of strength and a warning to the rest of the world. These are historically peaceful people, but they will never again run from a fight.

Looking forward in time, with fewer nations obscured behind curtains, iron or otherwise, the despots and their armies now have fewer places to operate where true genocide can be undetected. Nasty brutes will probably always occupy unstable thrones, and events can cascade quickly, but my faith is in the courage and nobility of humankind, and I believe true population-scale genocide is in humanity's past, not its future.

MILITARY OCCUPATION: SOCIETIES HELD IN ISOLATION

One painful example shows how s-DNA can be altered by prolonged military occupation. It begins in the deserts of what is now Saudi Arabia. From roughly the middle of the seventh century through the thirteenth, the Middle East was an epicenter of human accomplishment. The reason? Islam.

Islam spread quickly throughout the Middle East before moving across North Africa, and into Spain and Sicily. By the thirteenth century, Islam was present in India and even Southeast Asia. Islam became an empire, but not by force alone. Yes, powerful armies did move decisively in horse and camel cavalries, but the armies conquered armies; they did not destroy entire peoples. For the most part, Islamic rulers were tolerant and welcomed conversion to their faith. Arabic became the de-facto language and Islamic culture became a blending of Arab, Persian, Egyptian, and European traditions. Islam was a melting pot long before the American experiment began. The result was an era of stunning scientific, intellectual, and cultural achievements.

Consider these great ideas with a "Made by Muslims" stamp:

Innovation in Islamic

Coffee	Chess	Parachute	Trash cans
Shampoo	Distillation	Crankshaft	Surgery, hospital, medical schools and apothecary
Metal armor	College	Surveying equipment	Observatories
Windmill	Kerosene	Vaccinations	Fountain pen
Algebra and trigonometry	Soup	Carpet	Soap, shampoo and toothpaste
Bank checks	Rockets and torpedoes	Beauty parlor	Restaurant and three-course meal

The Society Inside Us

Five hundred years before Galileo, an Islamic astronomer determined that the Earth revolved around the Sun. The calculations of Islamic astronomers were so accurate that in the ninth century they calculated the Earth's circumference within 120 miles. Dig deeper into the roots of chemistry, architecture, mechanical engineering, medicine, geometry, and every other discipline that propels society forward, and you'll find Islamic innovations. This period—from the seventh to the thirteenth centuries—is often referred to as the Islamic Golden Age.

Now? Not so much.

Today, countries with majority Muslim populations fall below the global average on science- and technology-based innovation. What's worse, they've been stuck there for a long, long time. What happened?

The Crusades are usually seen by non-historians in the West as a regrettable assault on Arab nations in the name of Christianity. Most Westerners would be hard pressed to go deeper into the reasons or the timeline. In Arab societies, it's a different story. But first, a brief overview.

What we call "The Crusades" were actually a series of wars. They were launched by Christians in Western Europe to capture the Holy Land from the Muslims. The First Crusade (that's actually what it's called) began in 1095, just as Europe was emerging from the provincial Dark Ages. It could be argued that just as WWII helped lift the U.S. out of the Great Depression, the Crusades brought to Europe the higher standards of Eastern medicine and learning, the advances of Greek and Muslim culture, and even luxury goods like silk. Italy benefited greatly and the Italian Renaissance has its roots in the Crusades. By the mid-thirteenth century, the Crusades had shifted from large-scale military adventures to smaller incursions led by individual invaders.

The problem for Arab societies wasn't the wars—they lost, mostly, and suffered tremendous declines in their male populations, but all wars follow that basic script. What impacted the Arab nations most significantly during that period was the *occupation* by Western Europeans. The Crusaders never settled as residents in these conquered lands; they occupied them as overlords. For generations. Jerusalem remained in European hands for nearly 90 years, Palestine for over 190 years. And these occupiers weren't Richard the Lionhearted types either; they were either opportunistic or unfortunate. In the words of the Muslims from the period, the occupiers were "ruthless soldiers, semi-barbarous in nature, ignorant, and uncivilized." In response, Arab societies isolated their culture and science from outer influences and advances. Arab civilizations started to regress, displaying a growing lack of tolerance for intellectual debate and freethinking. They turned away from their time; something profound shifted in their s-DNA. Today with revolutions underway and decades-long regimes finally falling across North Africa and the Mideast, we may be seeing something equally profound: Muslim societies rejecting their inheritance of isolation and fundamentalism and moving once again toward vital global engagement.

EMIGRATION AND IMMIGRATION: SOCIETIES' PUSHES AND PULLS

While not as wrenching or immediate as armed conflict, emigration and immigration have a cumulative force that can reach even deeper into a nation's s-DNA. And no nation illustrates this better than the U.S., which has been a magnet for immigrants for so long that immigration itself has become a form of sustenance—we only notice it when there's not enough, or way too much. In the next chapter, we'll explore the immigrants' collective influence within the American s-DNA. Before that adventure begins, we'll take a quick detour into another nation that has become what it is because a lot of people showed up there from elsewhere: Australia.

IMMIGRATION OVERWHELMING

The native peoples of Australia were a diverse population of many tribal societies that today we lump together as Aboriginal Australians. Their numbers totaled 300,000, and when the first Europeans arrived in 1788, the locals didn't have a chance. Disease killed thousands; sheep and cattle pounded villages into dust; Aboriginal skulls were highly sought after by European universities. It was cultural genocide, if not actual human genocide. Then the prisoners started arriving.

During the late eighteenth and nineteenth centuries, large numbers of British convicts were transported to penal colonies in Australia. Demographers estimate that during the eighty-plus years that the colonies were functioning, more than 165,000 convicts were transported to Australia. What's more, the ill-mannered visitors were just beginning to arrive. Gold was discovered in Australia in 1851, and unleashed a gold rush that brought 370,000 immigrants in 1852 alone. By 1871 the total population had nearly quadrupled from 430,000 to 1.7 million people.

Prisoners and gold prospectors. Now there's a crew you'd want the keep away from your daughter...then, and now. Australia and New Zealand remain rough places for women. Australia has the third highest number of rapes per capita in the world, and the fourth most rapes in total. One percent of Australian women report being raped; in New Zealand it's 1.3 percent. Year after year, Australia is at the top—no, the shameful bottom—of the list for rape, date rape, and sexual assault. Maybe it's all the beer; only seven nations drink more beer per capita than Australians.

I'm not accusing all Australians of rape, or calling them drunks. I am revealing the data that strongly suggests there's something active at a population level that makes these crimes and this behavior more common than it is in nearly every other nation. The immigrants who arrived—shackles on their legs or fast fortunes in their eyes—shape the Australian s-DNA today. This is a testosterone-rich nation. They're tough and fiercely independent, but also among the first to enter the fray when there's a geopolitical wrong that needs to be righted. Australian infantry forces are some of the most effective and fearless, from the two World Wars to the conflicts in Iraq and Afghanistan. Australians played a significant role in the Korean War, and every modern peacekeeping or humanitarian mission has benefited from Australia's willingness to put boots on the ground where needed most.

EMIGRATION AND THE END OF THE RENAISSANCE

Now we turn to emigration—leaving home, and how a nation's s-DNA responds over time. Exhibit A: the Renaissance. Historians understand that the big chapters in the human story, periods like the Middle Ages or the Industrial Revolution, rarely have neat and tidy endpoints. They wind up slowly and wind down the same way. Historical distance blends those fuzzy transitions into dates that can fit on a timeline or in a textbook. The history books say the Renaissance began in the fourteenth century, about the time the barbarism of the Middle Ages had lost its charm and the bubonic plague was on the retreat. The Renaissance, regardless of when it began, was a period of great cultural and socio-economic advancement that spread from Italy across western Europe. The medieval agrarian societies were coalescing into city-states, beginning with Florence. In these new environments, gifted individuals could flourish even if they weren't nobles or men of the church. Leonardo da Vinci and Michelangelo have become the icons of the period, the original "Renaissance men."

And its end? The mid-seventeenth century is when the Renaissance ends on the timeline, but the "why" is just as fuzzy as the beginning. The Catholic Church and a succession of popes and princes, who had opened their deep pockets to build their cathedrals and commission the artists, were running out of spare gold pieces, thanks to the Italian wars of the 1500s. The Germans and Spaniards fought their way into Rome in 1527 and sacked it. At the same time, the cultural evolution that marked the Renaissance in Italy shifted north and west, giving it new life and new accents. Again, it's all fuzzy and seen only in the rear view mirror of historical context.

That said, I have another hunch about what brought the Renaissance to its final pages. It centers around another group of Renaissance men. . .not Leonardo or Michelangelo, but Christopher, Vasco, and Ferdinand.

Christopher Columbus, Vasco da Gama, and Ferdinand Magellan became the faces of discovery, and soon thereafter, opportunity. Their accomplishments in the late 1400s and throughout the 1500s opened more than new territory and trade routes; they also defined a new possibility for ordinary Europeans. It was contained in a single word: America.

The 1600s and 1700s saw the American continent become Europe West. A relative torrent of opportunistic, hardy, ambitious, and pious Europeans arrived. They were Europe's strivers—not its royalty, its richest, or its poorest. Those people stayed, their influence increasing (in the case of the noble and the affluent) and their sheer numbers multiplying (in the case of the poor.) The new Americans were Europe's "brain drain," leaving rings around the European tub that calcified into a population accustomed to a greater degree of state control. They would become the socialists of contemporary Europe because by the mid-1700s, the Renaissance had left the building.

THE INCREDIBLE SHRINKING IRELAND

In 1840 Ireland was the most densely populated nation in Europe; less than fifteen years later, nearly two million people—or about a quarter of the population—had emigrated to the United States alone. Hundreds of thousands more left for England and continental Europe. By 1890, two of every five Irish-born people were living *outside* Ireland. Of course, a lot of people were leaving Europe during this period. Sixty million Europeans departed for the Americas during the fifty years preceding World War I. But just as it is today, international travel is expensive, and poorer countries lost proportionately fewer workers than did more prosperous nations. Ireland was the exception—they were poor *and* they left in huge waves.

Ireland had been missed by the Industrial Revolution that was lifting European prosperity. In the mid 1800s, Ireland was essentially a densely populated agricultural nation. With epic crop failures and famines beginning in 1845, emigration was about survival. There simply were no other industries. Some demographers estimate that during the twentieth century over eighty million Irish citizens departed this small island that's about the size of West Virginia. Eighty million people.

I'm no scholar on the social psychology of Ireland, but I can say with some confidence that the s-DNA of the Irish people has been altered by the loss of so many people. The evidence? They keep leaving.

The Eurostat European Union statistics agency reported that Ireland's emigration rate in 2010 was the highest in the EU, almost double the second highest, Lithuania. Aside from the brief period from 1995 to 2000, when Ireland was nicknamed the "Celtic Tiger" and led the EU in immigration rates, Ireland has been among the most porous countries in Europe. A thousand citizens a month move to England alone, and Irish citizens have always left for other English-speaking countries like Australia, Canada, New Zealand and the U.S.—all relatively easy places to assimilate, but today's Irish are leaving for places that are not so easy, like China, Eastern Europe, and the Middle East.

Leaving Ireland has been encoded into the Irish s-DNA. It's a part of the Irish experience in ways that can't simply be explained by down economies, weak harvests, or even the dizzying opportunities that await in the New World.

Dizzying opportunities? Sounds fun—let's go.

Two

Immigration in America: How They Became Us

The Statue of Liberty is one crafty lady.

The words inscribed on her base may be one of the great misdirections in human history:

> *Give me your tired, your poor,*
> *Your huddled masses yearning to breathe free,*
> *The wretched refuse of your teeming shore.*

In other words, "Send us your losers and rejects; we'll make room, somehow."

Emma Lazarus, an American-born daughter of Portuguese immigrants, authored the inscription on the plaque. She penned it in 1883, in New York City, which locates Ms. Lazarus on the front row at the peak of America's immigrant parade. She saw firsthand the throbbing, thriving nation that those "huddled masses" were creating, and said, in effect, "This could be the greatest country in the world."

Of course, I'm speculating on the inner workings of Ms. Lazarus' mind, but she does give us another tantalizing clue to the America she really saw taking shape. Although the full text is an ornate jumble of fancy-pants prose, the title of the inscription practically thunders with ambition: The New Colossus.

Raw demographics alone tell us that the American character is rooted in European immigration. The seventy million immigrants who have arrived since the founding of the United States (formal records have only been kept since 1820) are responsible for the majority of the contemporary American population. If you are a white American, African American, Latino American, Asian American, or Arab American, then your family tree was planted on American soil by an immigrant.

Beginning in 1840, the largest human migration in history brought over thirty million immigrants to America. By the time it was interrupted in 1914 by World War I, America stood as the most prosperous nation on earth, and the most powerful. From the "tired and the poor," a Colossus had indeed emerged. But where, exactly, did it come from?

EUROPE: MODERN AND MEAN

The European mainland and British Isles never were large territories by contemporary American standards, and in the late 1700s they were starting to get even more cramped. From 1750 through the 1840s, Europe's population exploded. A hundred and forty million people became 250 million. The population nearly doubled in roughly three generations, with no territorial expansion. With a few exceptions on the more inhospitable northern edges, the continent was already settled from edge to edge. The practice of feudalism had faded or been outlawed altogether, but millions of Europeans still pulled their living from the soil. They were no longer serfs, but they sure were poor. Peasants we'd call them now, and in fact that's what they called themselves. Païsant is French for "one who shares the countryside." And in Ireland, England, Germany, Poland, and Italy, there was less and less countryside to share. Fortunately for many, the cities were calling.

The Industrial Revolution was probably less of a revolution and more of a technology-driven evolution. Yes, things were changing quickly, especially in London, Paris, Berlin, and other major cities, but the upheaval was less dramatic at a population level than the name suggests. In other words, the European s-DNA remained locked in an aristocratic configuration. Wealthy landowners often became wealthy industrialists with new textile enterprises. Or steam engine factories. Or iron foundries. For all the new wealth these industries were creating, it remained in the very old and very powerful families of Europe, many of which still wore crowns. The Industrial Revolution was making them richer, but another kind of revolution was making them nervous.

As the people of Europe gathered in these new industrial centers in the late 1700s and throughout the 1800s, they shared their dreams of autonomy—freedom of religion, freedom of speech, freedom from economic oppression. Some simply came to the cities for survival: craftspeople and artisans whose independent livelihoods, shaped over generations, were eroding or disappearing altogether. Low wages, dangerous work settings, and horrific housing conditions were grinding against some very proud spirits. Something wasn't working.

In America, the colonists had revolted and pushed British rule back onto the islands. The Treaty of Paris made it official in 1783. Then, a decade later, financially damaged by their support for the Americans, the French monarchy fell in a brutal and bloody revolt. The guillotine dropped on Queen Marie Antoinette's royal neck in 1793, and the governments in Russia, Germany, Turkey and others were not about join that party. Reform movements were smashed and reformers publicly executed. Ethnic intolerance was increasing as well, often fomented by oppressive governments as a way to shift anger away from their own policies. The term "pogrom" shows up in the early 1900s to describe what was taking place in Russia and Poland: massacres meant to expel and eliminate minority groups, particularly Jews. And "genocide" makes its linguistic debut as well, with the massacre of up to a million and a half Armenians by Ottoman authorities in 1915. By then the dream of leaving for America had taken root across the continent. Despite the turmoil and carnage that WWI was about to unleash, a modern Europe was taking shape. And yet for millions it held all the promise of Medieval Europe.

AMERICA TRANSFORMED, IN TWO MASSIVE WAVES

Demographers identify two major periods of American immigration, from 1800 to 1880, and from 1880 to the beginning of WWI. What define each are the origin of the immigrants and the scale of their numbers.

From the first settlements in the 1400s through the nation's birth, America had accumulated just over two million people. By 1800, there were 5.3 million, many of them immigrants. But the big waves were just beginning. In the early decades of the 1800s, American population was growing by 50 percent each decade. From 1840 to 1880, ten million or more Europeans entered the country, mostly from northern and western Europe. Scandinavians settled in the Midwest and northern cities; Germans in New York, Baltimore, Cincinnati, St. Louis, and Milwaukee; British and Irish in Boston, New York, and other northeastern communities. There were fifty million Americans then, and Eastern and Southern Europe's turn had finally come. Beginning in 1880, Russians, Poles, Hungarians, Greeks, Ukrainians, and Italians dominated the immigrant ship's manifest—twenty million or more from 1880 to 1900.

Here's a telling fact: In 1880, 250,000 Jews lived in New York City, most of them from western Europe, like inscription author Emma Lazarus mentioned earlier, herself a Sephardic Jew whose family immigrated from Portugal. When the eastern Europeans arrived from

Russia, Poland, and Hungary, they upped the Jewish population of New York City to nearly 1.5 million—a quarter of the entire city's population.

Knowing the raw numbers and the context around them is essential for understanding the scale of immigration, but let's step away from the demographics for a few moments. Because numbers aren't people. They can't measure ambition or inventiveness or the fire in a belly that burns inside a family for generations. The American s-DNA was cooking in the melting pot, and the world had never experienced anything like it.

THE AMERICA THEY BUILT, THE AMERICANS WE BECAME

You've probably seen some of the black-and-white photos of immigrants just off the boat in Ellis Island. What do you see in those faces? Indeed many do look "tired and poor." That's because they were—the steamships that delivered them across the Atlantic were hardly luxury vessels, and many had saved for years just to afford the ticket. But look a little closer, because behind the fatigue and the meager finances are the first strands of the American s-DNA, which actually began to form before they had even left home.

Think for a moment about the last time you moved into a new home—it was exhausting, and exciting, and maybe a little frightening, but short on true existential drama. Not so for these American immigrants. They weren't merely "moving"; they were turning their back on everything that home had been. It was profoundly difficult, even for the most optimistic and enthusiastic. Feeling restless or even dissatisfied wasn't enough. They *longed*; they *dreamed*. And in those dreams they would find new brothers and sisters in the immigrant reception areas of Ellis Island. I'm sure it wasn't kumbaya—they were still Italian, Polish, and Hungarian—but they were beginning to see the shared territory between them. . .a story they had told themselves over and over about America, and the people they could become here.

History.com has a fantastic set of videos on their Ellis Island page. I highly recommend you peel away and spend some time there, and keep watching for Renee Burkoff. She arrived in 1922, and sings a verse that her shipmates sang when the Statue of Liberty was finally in sight:

> *In America, life is golden.*
> *In America the flowers are more beautiful.*
> *In America the world is much better*
> *And that's what I'm longing to be, my dear.*

Let's unpack that idea of "longing to be better" because it contains so much that's essential for our understanding of the American s-DNA.

THE RAW MATERIAL OF AMERICAN S-DNA

The American recipe has a few very distinct ingredients:

1. **Risk-taking**—These immigrants took enormous risks in leaving home and starting over. Scientists tell us now that risk-taking has a recognized genetic component, and it must have been shared by millions of immigrants.
2. **Independence**—New immigrants may have had family or friends waiting here, but none of them came here to be taken in and taken care of. And imagine the immigrants who stepped of the boat and knew absolutely no one—call them independent with a capital *I*.

3. **Opportunism**—America earned its name as the "Land of Opportunity" because seeking opportunities is a constant in the immigrant story.

4. **An ethic of hard work**—Work wasn't easy on either side of the Atlantic, but the immigrants arriving in America believed that their hard work could deliver something more than mere survival.

5. **Pride**—Sure, immigrants certainly had a group pride tied to ethnicity, but these immigrants were building something new on top of their roots.

6. **Inventiveness**—Remember that old saying that "Necessity is the mother of invention"? Well, welcome to necessity. These new Americans were inventing their nation—the businesses, the cities, the churches, the governments. The inventor was an early American archetype.

7. **Motivation, rather than education**—The most educated Europeans were the ones who stayed behind. American immigrants knew they'd learn what they needed to learn by succeeding. Of course, many failed, but lack of education was rarely seen as the reason.

See anything familiar? Those traits *are* the American s-DNA, and they are as vital today as they were then.

THE CONTEMPORARY EXPRESSION OF AMERICAN S-DNA

Later chapters dig deep into how these traits are shaping the global economy, in the U.S. and elsewhere. But let's quickly close the loop and see how the traits became actions:

1. **Risk-taking**—The Greeks invented the Olympics; Americans invented the X-Games. And the first exchange for publicly traded

stocks. Win or lose, we admire those who risk it all. That's highly unusual in contemporary Europe and in Asian nations. "Nothing ventured, nothing gained" is a purely American idiom.

2. **Independence**—America's party day is Independence Day. It's what we admire and what we teach. The U.S.'s participation in the League of Nations and then the United Nations has always been contentious.

3. **Opportunism**—Americans create more businesses per capita than any other nation. The entrepreneur was created here, and although they'll complain today about how our government makes it harder to launch a new venture, they should try it in Europe—the U.S. looks like the Wild West again.

4. **An ethic of hard work**—Traveling salesman-turned-philosopher Elbert Hubbard said, "Luck is the tenacity of purpose." Most Americans believe that even luck has to be handmade. Today, we work longer weeks and take fewer vacations than any other developed nation. That isn't always a good thing, but we're not here to judge, merely to recognize.

5. **Pride**—Pride can border on nationalism and even demagoguery. You see it on bumper stickers, concert stages, and on flagpoles in suburban front yards. We may be interested in our Irish heritage, but we're proud to be American.

6. **Inventiveness**—Today we call it innovation, and it has permanent residence in places like Silicon Valley, Detroit, and even Hollywood.

7. **Motivation rather than education**—Americans respect the well educated, but they admire the self-made. And if someone has overcome the disadvantages of a lesser education and succeeded on the grand stage—guys like the late Steve Jobs—we make them our icons. Which is not to suggest the U.S. de-values education—American colleges are the best in the world, and magnets for millions of U.S. and international students.

Before we leave this chapter, let's return to the early immigrants and specifically what they meant to a new nation. There's more than just economic and cultural history here; there's s-DNA wrapping tighter and tighter around every American today.

IMMIGRANTS PUSHED THE FRONTIER WEST

American became defined by both the Atlantic and the Pacific during the period when European immigration was at its peak. (It's time to include Chinese immigrants in the conversation too. Their numbers were smaller, their geographic spread was narrower, and their assimilation was minimal, but their influence should not be overlooked. After Chinese immigrants helped build the transcontinental railroad, they took major roles in California agriculture, fisheries, and as merchants.) Pushing the American frontier westward were German and Scandinavian immigrants and their direct descendants. As they surveyed and settled the new American West, they were also embedding into the American s-DNA traits such as courage, self-reliance, and faith that a better place awaited through the next mountain pass.

IMMIGRANTS WERE THE MUSCLE OF AMERICA'S NEW INDUSTRIES

In the early 1800s, Irish immigrants worked as laborers in cities and were the major source of manpower in the construction of canals, railroads, and roads across the northeast U.S. You've probably heard the lore about how employers would write on their "Help Wanted" signs, "Irish Need Not Apply." Nothing but historical foam, says Richard Jensen, a retired professor of history at the University of Chicago. He writes:

The fact that Irish vividly "remember" No Irish Need Apply (NINA) signs is a curious historical puzzle. There are no contemporary or retrospective accounts of a specific sign at a specific location. No particular business enterprise is named as a culprit. No historian, archivist, or museum curator has ever located one; no photograph or drawing exists. No other ethnic group complained about being singled out by comparable signs. Only Irish Catholics have reported seeing the sign in America—no Protestant, no Jew, no non-Irish Catholic has reported seeing one. This is especially strange since signs were primarily directed toward these others: the signs said that employment was available here and invited Yankees, French-Canadians, Italians and any other non-Irish to come inside and apply. The business literature, both published and unpublished, never mentions NINA or any policy remotely like it. The newspapers and magazines are silent. The courts are silent. There is no record of an angry youth tossing a brick through the window that held such a sign. Have we not discovered all of the signs of an urban legend?

Professor Jensen believes the story is a relic from England, where the Irish were indeed discriminated against. In America, NINA was nothing more than an odd victimization myth and was uttered in public as the chorus to a popular drinking song. America was Irish, and German and Polish and Italian. And it was hiring.

European immigrants and their children filled the garment sweatshops of New York, the coalfields of Pennsylvania, and the stockyards of Chicago. In 1900, roughly 75 percent of the populations of many large cities were composed of immigrants and their descendants, including New York, Chicago, Boston, Cleveland, San Francisco, Buffalo, Milwaukee, and Detroit.

Some of these lives may have looked little different from the laborers in Dickens' London, but there were differences. In 1800s America, trade unions were gaining strength, and even early labor strikes succeeded in increasing pay and improving working conditions. These men, alongside some women, worked hard. They knew the value of their labor to a growing nation, and were gaining a sense that collective action could reward them and their families; it wasn't just about a fatter pay envelope, it was about a better life. New ideas were becoming encoded into the American s-DNA: a collective pride not defined by ethnicity alone and a belief that working together could change the nation in meaningful ways.

IMMIGRANTS WERE THE OWNERS OF AMERICAN SMALL BUSINESS

Immigrants in America created the formula of modern small business: modest capital investment multiplied by hard work and intelligent adaptation equals financial security. Although European immigrants brought it to life, that's not a European idea. It's made in America, and it endures in America. Small business was and remains the most important sector of the American economy.

And immigrants continue to own their share of this sector. In every U.S. census from 1880 onward, immigrants accounted for a greater percentage of small business owners than natives. American s-DNA gained a few more traits: independence, vision, and a willingness to sacrifice in the short term when there's a larger dream within reach.

IMMIGRANTS HELPED AMERICA ENDURE ITS GREATEST TRIAL

No contemporary challenge—financial, political, or cultural—compares in the wrenching despair of the Civil War. Those events are well documented; it's undoubtedly the most thoroughly investigated and analyzed period in American history, and the more I learn about it, the more my appreciation grows for the immigrants who went to fight for their new home.

The vast majority of European immigrants that arrived in the early 1800s opposed slavery. They came here to be free, not to enslave. The struggle for abolition included large numbers of immigrants, even in leadership roles. In 1860, immigrants turned out in massive numbers for Abraham Lincoln. Without their votes, some historians argue, there would have never been a Lincoln presidency. Ponder that for a while.

When secession became war, immigrants were among the first to enlist. Historians estimate that of the approximately two million men who suited up for the Union Army, over 400,000 were immigrants. Ponder that, too: In a war to save the soul of America, nearly a quarter of the warriors weren't even born here.

What those immigrants inserted into the American s-DNA is probably beyond words, but I'll try: a willingness to fight for ideals, not just territory.

EMIGRANTS ALLOWED EUROPE TO DEEPEN WHAT MAKES THEM EUROPEAN

No analysis of immigrants' impact would be complete without looking back at what they left behind, specifically what happened (or didn't happen) when European emigrants became American immigrants. Is it a coincidence that institutionally-oriented, liberal Europe began to take shape in the eighteenth and nineteenth centuries? I don't think so. Millions of Europe's risk-taking, independent, and opportunistic people said, "See ya" to those European structures that, depending on the period, were church-dominated societies, aristocracies, or even military-oriented dictatorships. The Renaissance, Europe's 200-year high-water mark in the arts, literature, philosophy, politics, and science had run out of steam by the end of the seventeenth century. Or, about the time the New World was opening for the next generation of cultural experimenters.

No matter where the retrospective lens is pointed, you see European nations where hierarchy and class defined the reality. Tradition, status quo, and old money never had much patience for independent thinkers bent on disturbing the peace and disrupting the order. So with fewer of them around to cause trouble, the course of history moved on a reasonably predictable course: Monarchies evolved into liberal democracies, and governments arose as the dominant institutions. Their assumed role? Take care of everybody: make it hard to fail and don't play favorites. In fact, let's enact national policy as a single regional body and trade the same currency. Liberal democracies can be wonderful places to raise a family and ride out a retirement. High taxation buys a lot of government services. Europeans are content, especially now that all those Americans are gone.

WE ARE ALL THIS AND MORE

Americans became Americans not by birthright, but by arriving and striving and believing. For all of its geographic advantages, America is less about place and more about something closer to soul. Harry Truman said, "You know that being an American is more than a matter of where your parents came from. It is a belief that all men are created free and equal and that everyone deserves an even break."

The immigrant's influence on the American character is not a simple story. I've compressed layered and nuanced histories into compact form. The historian in me wants to go deeper, while the economist in me wants more context: How does American s-DNA position it in global economic terms? And specifically, what can we determine about America's future by looking at another nation that makes our 300 or so years of s-DNA accumulation look like a thin veneer on a very thick table?

Three

China Now: Communal and Conflicted

As China ascends in the public imagination—both as a model of energized consumerism and as a feared landlord to America's financial system—it's vital to understand the societal DNA of China. It's not an immigration story, but there's a lot of conflict and drama. To see it, we need to spend some time under the hood of the Chinese personality.

You've seen those timelines that show the epochs of dinosaurs compared to the skinny sliver of time in which modern humans walked the Earth. It's both amazing and humbling: Yes, we've accomplished a lot, and no, we really haven't demonstrated much staying power. Either reaction also works when you compare the history of the U.S. to China's. China has dynasties. America has administrations.

The Xia Dynasty is usually identified as the first Chinese dynasty, and it endured from 2,000 B.C. until 1,500 B.C. Five hundred years, and it's only the first. The name "China" had been around for a couple of hundred years of B.C. That was probably the work of the Qin Dynasty, which is pronounced, "Chin," and gets credit for creating a centralized government that instituted a common written language and currency. The Qins also started building the Great Wall, perhaps the first global security infrastructure project. (It actually may have been built for another reason entirely, but we'll get to that.) The Great Wall definitely puts a notch in the timeline that marks the beginning of a sovereign China. And remember, the calendar is just showing roughly 200 B.C. China isn't just old; it's ancient, a fact that's critical to understanding the Chinese s-DNA.

The generational accumulation of character traits is not only deep in China; it's also dense in the same way layers of sediment become layer of rock in geological time. For a while, sediment can shift and settle further. Once it's rock it doesn't settle, and it only shifts when the earth shakes it loose. The Chinese s-DNA has solidified into traits that are deeply ingrained in the Chinese personality. Said simply, the Chinese s-DNA is as strong—and as flexible—as rock.

The immigration that has kept the American s-DNA in a state of relative fluidity hasn't shaped China to nearly the same degree. Of course, China is a giant piece of real estate—roughly the size of the continental U.S.— with thousands of miles that border other nations. Millions of Chinese people can probably trace their roots back to Mongolia, or Nepal, or Korea. Yet it's almost certainly not measured in decades or with statements like, "my great grandparents came here from. . ." We're talking hundreds of years and scores of generations—that's outside of genealogy and more like archeology. Today the largest ethnic group in China, totaling over 90 percent of the population, is Han Chinese. They're Chinese people who came from Chinese people who came from Chinese people who... You get it. What's more, during the seventeenth, eighteenth, and about half of the nineteenth centuries, China was effectively closed for business, especially with Europe. Except for a limited foreign trade through the city of Canton, China isolated itself: minimal commercial influence and virtually no immigration. Just think about that. In the exact same period that the American s-DNA was cooking into its current form, China's was frozen in place.

So what *did* give shape to the Chinese s-DNA? Maybe the real question isn't "what" but "who."

HOW CONFUCIUS CREATED CHINA

In 551 B.C., Confucius was born in northeastern China. He grew up in a poor region and with a poor family, but his ambition was overflowing and his timing was perfect. China was in the midst of an unsettled time; multiple factions were fighting for political dominance and new philosophies were rising. Confucius seized the moment. Beginning around the age of 50, he took on the role of cultural provocateur and began spreading a set of very specific ideas about how people should act and societies should operate. For over a decade Confucius traveled throughout China, talking to rulers and peasants alike on how to improve Chinese society. He never saw the influence of his ideas, but by roughly 400 B.C., or about 150 years after his birth, Confucianism was recognized as the dominant cultural ideology in China, thus stamping the die for the Chinese s-DNA that we see today. By any human measure, the man had an impact. Let's look at its dimensions.

Confucianism recognizes five cardinal virtues:

1. Benevolence in terms of sympathy for others (*jen*)
2. Duty reflected in the shame felt after doing something wrong (*yi*)
3. Manners, propriety, and feelings of deference (*li*)
4. Wisdom, in terms of discerning right and wrong (*chih*)
5. Loyalty and good faith (*hsin*)

All good things for sure, but it's the next layer down where the particular s-DNA of China starts to take shape.

Confucius was not concerned about individual rights. What he cared about most was the collective wellbeing of society. Beginning with the father, and extending upward to the Emperor, Confucius promoted the virtues of courtesy, selflessness, obedience, respect, diligence, communal obligation, working for a common good, and social harmony. Each was reinforced by a code of behavior that honored and obeyed the father and the mother, the elders, and the leaders.

The Confucian code of was enforced by social means, not laws. Forget "an eye for an eye" brutality. Under Confucian codes, accused criminals were ostracized and humiliated, along with their families. Confucius said: "If you govern by regulations and keep them in order by punishment, the people will avoid trouble but have no sense of shame. If you govern them by moral influence, and keep them in order by a code of manners, they will have a sense of shame and will come to you of their own accord." (Shame is a powerful societal force, and we'll explore it more later in the chapter.)

Confucian codes made high-density living livable. While China is about the same size as the U.S., "wide open spaces" and "give me some elbow room" were never a part of their lexicon. China's population was, and is, highly concentrated in urban areas. They've always lived in close proximity to their neighbors, and have been communal by the strictest definition of the word. By assuming Confucian codes of conduct, the Chinese made high-density living work. Disruptions and disorder are magnified in urban spaces, and neighbors take charge if there's no other authority around. I'm speaking broadly here, because it's as true in Confucius' China as it is in today's New York City. The social contracts set limits on what's expected and tolerated. It's just that in China, the contracts are written in the blood of a thousand ancestors.

Confucius insisted on formal rules for how people relate. The third cardinal virtue of *li* defines how people are supposed to behave toward one another. In Confucian code, the dominant person receives respect and obedience from the subordinate person. However, obedience doesn't mean one has given up humanity; the dominant person is supposed to reciprocate with love, goodwill, support, and affection. What could possibly go wrong with that? Well, keep reading.

CONFUCIANISM UNDER COMMUNISM: VIOLENTLY AGREEING

The People's Republic of China was born in 1949, when communist Chinese rebels led by Mao Zedong defeated the nationalist government of Chiang Kai-shek. Mao came to power trashing Confucianism with every proclamation, claiming that it locked China in the "feudal mentality" of the past. Mao had another idea on who should be receiving the respect traditionally reserved for fathers and elders: the state. As it turns out, it wasn't much of a shift going from Confucian ideals to communist laws—the s-DNA was already in place. What looked like oppression to the West was actually a scaled up version of a centuries-old cultural mindset. Short of turning this into a textbook or a screed, I offer two heartbreaking examples of how communist authoritarianism pitched its tent on the bedrock of Chinese s-DNA.

The Great Leap Forward was Mao's first big idea. He believed China had the muscle and might to build an industrial base unrivaled anywhere in the modern world, and nothing is more industrial than steel. To make it, the Chinese people were relocated on a massive scale, from rural villages to giant communes. The Leap peaked in the late 1950s, and historians estimate that 700 million people had been placed in communes. Let me say that number again: 700 million people. All of whom handed everything they owned to the state, and went to work making steel and industrial products made of steel.

As industrial processes go, steel is relatively easy to make. The communes were kicking it out in unprecedented quantities from the so-called "backyard furnaces." The party officials were delighted with the tons and tons of steel stacking up. But what was missing in their rosy reports back to Mao was the quality of the product—steel is easy; high-grade steel is infinitely more difficult, and well beyond the capabilities of a backyard furnace anywhere but maybe Pittsburgh. In 1959 it all started to fall apart—literally. The farm machinery produced in the communes fell to pieces when they hit the hard reality of dirt. Structural steel used to construct buildings, many of which were in the communes themselves, started to collapse in heaps. Meanwhile, back at the farms, nothing much was happening, again literally.

Fewer farmers now worked the fields and the weather wasn't helping. Some areas flooded; some endured drought. Everywhere the harvests were down and people were starving. As many as forty-five million Chinese starved to death between 1959 and 1962. Can you imagine any government surviving if they had forced most of the people into labor camps and then let millions starve to death? Guess what? They weren't even done.

The Cultural Revolution was Mao's big second act, and it played straight into China's s-DNA in its most violent expressions. Mao's star had dimmed considerably after the Great Leap fell flat. He imposed his authority anew, beginning in 1965, by attacking the privileged class of engineers, economists, scientists, writers, artists, university faculty, and even factory managers. Mao and his party accused them of leading China away from its humble roots and communist ideals. Sounds like the typical rhetorical bombs of full-contact politics, right? What happened next was actually the most vicious kind of war.

The Red Guards were any group that banded together in service of Mao's vision of a "classless society." Some were official army and police, but many were nothing more than angry, violent mobs. Innocent people were paraded in front of screaming crowds where they were beaten or killed. Children denounced and attacked their parents. In a Beijing school, the students beat a principal to death with nail-studded planks. Oh, and it was an all-girls school. Past the horrors of neighbor-against-neighbor strife, monasteries were destroyed, priceless works of antiquity and ancient art were smashed, and millions of young people were forced from urban areas into the countryside, where they had few relevant skills. It's hard to know how many people were killed and how many died from the conditions

China Now: Communal and Conflicted

that were spawned. Some estimates say a few million; others claim as many as 30 million died, which would rank The Cultural Revolution as one of the worst genocides of the twentieth century.

As discussed earlier, genocide can alter s-DNA, but that takes several generations to show up. The Cultural Revolution ended in 1968; many millions of Chinese citizens experienced it personally. It remains a brutal tear in the social fabric of China, made all the more disturbing by the way that justifying violence perverted the deep tenants of Confucianism. And in its aftermath, there has been no South African style Truth and Reconciliation Committee, and very little legal action at all. Tormenters and victims went back to work, sometimes side by side. By the 1970s, Mao was dead but Confucianism was thriving, and China was plowing into the next grand plan which has become the economic juggernaut you see today.

A FEW WORDS ON SHAME

Earlier in the chapter, I introduced the Confucian code of preserving social order through shame. It bears further exploration here because it has resonance in the day-to-day manifestations of Chinese s-DNA, specifically how a shame-based culture differs from American culture, which psychologists describe as guilt based. Take a look at the following comparisons and see whether you agree.

	Shame-based society	Guilt-based society
I'm innocent!	If we believe you did it anyway, you are dishonored.	If we believe you did it anyway, you must prove your innocence.
OK, I did it.	We'll punish you and dishonor your family.	We'll punish you.
I did it, but you don't know.	You won't be dishonored and nothing will change.	You must carry your guilt alone.

In a shame-based society, what other people believe is more powerful than what you know to be true. It places a premium on preserving honor versus knowing the truth. Appearing innocent is more important than actually being innocent, which can give rise to all kinds of shadowy wrong-doing. An un-accused criminal in a guilt-based society may confess before the same un-accused criminal does in a shame-based society. After all, why confess if you've already escaped the worst of it?

In a shame-based society, suspicion can be enough to convict. Group think (or mob mentality) rules, and the facts of the case matter less, if at all. An accusation—especially if it comes from someone in a powerful position—may be all the evidence needed to destroy a person's reputation and the sully the name of his or her family. Underground and closed societies like the Mafia are often shame-based, but shame also shows up in families, workplaces, and sorority houses everywhere, including the in U.S. Japan is definitely shame-based. And China? Look at Confucius and everything that's happened in China since his campaign of social engineering took root.

Shame, or more broadly, the approval of others, is a core element in the Chinese s-DNA, and there are two distinct reactions to it. One is to accept it—to dishonor others when called upon and to submit to personal dishonor in all its unfairness. It's the sweatshop worker who commits suicide because she can't keep up, shaming herself and the hard workers on her line. The other reaction is to deny it, or rather to counter it with a strident insistence that *"Today's* China is not *that* China and we're claiming our rightful role as the modern world's dominant nation."

Sudden wealth can set off all kinds of unusual behaviors—just ask a lottery winner. And political forces *can* re-shape nations to some degree. Communism as a political force took hold in the

China Now: Communal and Conflicted

Russian Revolution of 1917. It hasn't even reached its hundredth birthday. Confucianism has it beat by about 2400 years. China *is* Confucius wearing a communist cloak and just starting to make it big in the capitalist world. Another way to say it: China is a colossal contradiction. And while their contradictions may confound the West, it's just another day in the land of silkworms and giant pandas.

CONTEMPORARY CONTRADICTIONS: IT'S HOW THEY ROLL

Much has been made of the contradictions between China's communist government and its fevered capitalist impulses. But clashing opposites can also generate a paradoxical power—the very things that confound a Westerner are just as quickly celebrated by the Chinese. Two examples, one spiritual and the other political:

To remain whole, yield somewhat,
To become straight, let yourself look bent.
To become full, seem hollow.
Seem tattered now, that you can be renewed.
Those that have little, can get more,
To have plenty is to be confused.

From the Tao Te Ching

Changes in society are due chiefly to the development of
the internal contradictions in society, that is, the contradiction between
the productive forces and the relations of production,

the contradiction between classes and the contradiction between the old and the new; it is the development of these contradictions that pushes society forward and gives the impetus for the supersession of the old society by the new.

From Mao's "On Contradiction"

Contradictions and all, China is a commercial colossus, thanks in part to a fully supportive communist government. But cracks are starting to show, and in the next chapter we'll poke at a few.

Four

Mommy and Her Chinese Teenager

This chapter begins with pride, angst, and controversy. All three swirled around *Battle Hymn of the Tiger Mother*, a book by Amy Chua. Her 2011 memoir polarized parents, educators, and cultural observers. The media couldn't get enough of her, or Americans' reactions to her parenting practices. You didn't even need to read it—in fact, I haven't—to pick up the storyline: The author raised her two daughters under strict rules that drained all the fun out of childhood. Instead of sleepovers and play dates, Mom hammered the kids with intense daily sessions on the piano or violin, and hours of extra academics. In interviews, Ms. Chua defended her Asian-style parenting as an antidote to the passive Western parenting that's more concerned with the kids' self-esteem than their achievement. She came just short of calling us lazy.

Depending on when you're reading this, it's possible that you can still hear the shrieking from defensive parents who attacked the methods (and the mom) as not just "extreme" but "insane." You still might also be able to sense the national handwringing as people used the book as one more piece of evidence that China is destined to drink our milkshake.

Without a doubt, *Tiger Mother* fit conveniently into the broader narrative of Chinese superiority that this book is working to dismantle. It's not fair for me to comment on Ms. Chua's parenting; scroll through the Amazon.com reviews and read what the book's readers have to report: righteous fury and dreadful predictions.

But there's another Chinese mother that I believe readers should get to know better. Let's just call her "Mommy."

China is an exuberant but untested capitalist. Throughout the first two decades of the century, they've posted spectacular (if occasionally specious) GDP numbers. In 2010 they overtook Japan as the world's second largest economy. We're going to get underneath that growth in the pages ahead, but first some historical perspective.

China's emergence as a global economic player began waaaay back in 1979 when Deng Xiaoping took the reins after the collapse of the Cultural Revolution, and began to implement market-oriented reforms. Deng hit the circuit just like any other enthusiastic economic development pitchman. He brought his China 2.0 road show to the U.S., where he talked to Boeing in Seattle and Coca-Cola in Atlanta. He toured the Space Center in Houston, and sat down with President Carter, along with a few senators and congressmen.

Back in China, Deng slowly implemented reforms—too slowly for many Chinese, eager to participate in the promised free markets. Many were students who dreamed of political change, including taking a meaningful role in government. Their agendas mixed with a simmering stew of other grievances in June of 1989, and they all headed for Beijing's Tiananmen Square. Throughout the spring of 1989 were protests, boycotts, hunger strikes, even a few small riots. Deng Xiaoping's government found itself engaged in a crisis on multiple fronts, internally and internationally. The West was watching to see what this new China could tolerate from its suddenly vocal and agitated citizens. The answer came on June 4, when the tanks rolled in.

The estimates of people killed and injured in the Tiananmen Square massacre vary wildly. 10,000 dead is about as high as they go; the Chinese government says 241 dead and 7,000 wounded. The truth is likely somewhere in the middle, and yet it's just *one man* who probably best represents Tiananmen Square to Americans. Do you remember the video? A column of tanks is moving along a mostly deserted street until it reaches a man in a white shirt, and stops. The man stands motionless, then waves his arm angrily. The tank is immense, and just feet away. It could crush him in seconds, but stands frozen, then tries to maneuver around him as the man moves in front again, and then again. Eventually, we see several people pull him away.

His identity remains a mystery. *TIME* magazine named him one of the 100 Most Influential People of the Twentieth Century. Many China observers believe he was taken prisoner and promptly executed. It's also hard to know just how deeply Chinese society was torn. Chinese s-DNA has three thousand years of accumulated deference to power; surely a few awful days and one man weren't enough to disrupt it. What's more, had any one man so completely represented everything that China is *not*?

Inside China, not surprisingly, the events have been wiped from the history books. Quite effectively, it seems: In 2006 an American documentary crew showed the images of Tank Man to a group of present-day students, and it meant nothing to them. One asked if it was a parade. The Tiananmen Square protestors failed to produce a movement that lasted or an ideology than inspired. No individual or group since has been able to generate even modest political structures that might become a viable alternative to China's single-party government. To my eye, that's Chinese s-DNA returning to the default setting of respect for authority, even as it demonstrates its authoritarian nature.

After Tiananmen, foreign capital stayed away for a few years, as did the tourists, but by the early 1990s China was back in business. And that's when China's economic "miracle" really started to spin up.

If you've been keeping track, China 2.0 had been around for about a decade before Tiananmen and now has been another two decades since. From my perch here in late 2011, that's about thirty years. Thirty *whole* years. You really can't help being flat out amazed at what they've accomplished in that time; I certainly am. You also absolutely can't lose sight of China's inexperience in contemporary capital markets and global trade. It's one area where the U.S. is the graybeard and China is the kid.

Hey! Who wants to go for a bike ride??

GETTING ALL WOBBLY ON TWO WHEELS

Remember learning to ride a bike? No matter how quickly you took to it, mastery didn't come before a few falls. You know *now* that a skinned knee or banged up elbow is just part of learning, but the very first time it happened? Whaaaaa! That fall sent you running straight to Mommy. It sure did me. And then, bandage on, the fear fades and excitement returns. You're out the door and back on the bike. Later that week there was another tumble, and then another. Maybe Nurse Mom was called in, or maybe not. Because c'mon...the other kids are all standing there, and besides, it's already starting to feel better. Mom doesn't even need to know. Let's ride!

Now, let's say the kid on the bike is China, 1.3 billion new riders on the unfamiliar capitalist street. Yes, they're fast learners, and are pushing the pedals as if they were born on a bike. But know this: They *are* going to take a spill. And even if it's not serious enough to break major economic bones, they are going to do what every newbie does: they're going to run back to Mommy so she can make it better.

I'm not inferring that the Chinese are sissies. Given how long they've lasted and prospered, quite the opposite. They're simply new capitalists on new bikes, and sooner or later they're gonna crash. When they do, they are going to turn to the only Mommy they have now, the Communist Party leaders, and they're going to say, "Fix this."

The same thing happens in mature economies, too. Take the crisis of late 2008 when the housing bubble burst and a truly frightening series of events began to cascade. The big American banks turned to the U.S. Treasury and said, essentially, "Fix this." But we've been on that bike a long time and have endured enough spills to know that the bike isn't the problem. And before the fixing was even finished in Washington D.C., the banks were cleaning up their books and getting back in gear. Capitalism didn't crash, though a few reckless capitalists did.

When the capitalist bike goes down in China, what then? The very idea of even riding the bike could be thrown into question. Will we see a severe tightening of credit from the free-lending banks? A sudden frugality by their free-spending middle class? A hasty exit for Western brands and foreign investment? Even if they do retreat to a more overt paternalism, the social dislocation will be heartbreaking. That first fall, or series of falls, could have momentous implications within China and globally, and nobody knows what they will be. So if we're going speculate, let's be a little smarter about it. Let's *not* focus on the post-crash carnage and instead take a close look at what we *can* see ahead: the specific road conditions that the new capitalist rider is blasting toward.

I sure hope he's wearing a helmet.

Bump One: A Massively Overheated Real Estate Market

The common perception that Chinese people have a knack for math is about to take a hit. There are an estimated 65 million vacant housing units in China, reports the website *Seeking Alpha* in a not-so-subtly titled piece, "The Mother of All Bubbles." There's also the

2.2 million square foot South China Mall with space for 2,100 stores, which sits completely vacant. And it's one of many.

Across China you can find brand new cities with nobody home. Sprawling university campuses and no students. See for yourself with a Google search for "China + ghost towns," you'll see downright eerie videos on YouTube and satellite images that look like the fabled neutron bomb had been dropped. Turns out *nothing* has dropped, including prices. Notice the change below in font color—at the end of the first line it becomes gray instead of black. I saw this as I was editing, and changed it often, but because it's a document issue rather than an editing issue I didn't focus on it. I believe I queried about it, but couldn't tell you where for sure. I don't know what will happen to it as the document goes to print.

According to an IMF report cited by the *Telegraph* in December of 2010, "home prices in Shenzhen, Shanghai, Beijing, and Nanjing seem increasingly disconnected from fundamentals. Prices are 22 times disposable income in Beijing, and 18 times in Shenzhen, compared to eight in Tokyo. The U.S. bubble peaked at 6.4 and has since dropped 4.7. The price-to-rent ratio in China's eastern cities has risen by over 200 percent since 2004." With prices that high and rising, everyone wants in on that party, right? Apparently so.

Individual investors in China don't have a lot of good options. Savings rates aren't keeping up with China's 5 percent inflation rate; Chinese equities are extremely volatile given that every industry and every sector is still developing; and investing in international securities is limited by government capital controls. So what's left? Real estate. To the new members of the Chinese upper and middle classes, real estate speculation is the investment of choice. It's not uncommon for people to own five units or more, all of them unoccupied. Low rental prices make being a landlord more hassle than it's worth. Even non-real estate businesses are shifting their investments away from manufacturing and into property and development. Somebody is massively exposed here.

A lot of residential transactions are essentially cash deals. Buyers (speculators, remember) place deposits that the developer leverages for construction financing. The developer then carries the buyer for a shockingly short period of time—usually a year or two—and the note is paid in full. Traditional mortgage products are increasing in usage, but the down payment is typically 30 percent or more. Chinese homebuyers have invested everything in these properties. *Exposed: buyers.* Local governments are scooping up their share of the froth too; they are selling their land and financing the construction. In one report, 11 percent of China's total outstanding debt is held by local government funding vehicles, or LGFVs. *Exposed: local governments.* To keep the GDP engine chugging out its double-digit growth, the national government tells banks to lend for development even if developers can't demonstrate a need. Hence the ghost cities and empty malls. *Exposed: developers and banks.*

As you can see, exposure is not limited to a single sector, like finance. That's good, usually. We saw what can happen in the U.S. when no-cash-down homebuyers drive prices—and then just walk away. It's a good thing to have skin in the game as long as the game is going well, but right now China is overbuilt and overpriced. The game's getting kind of crazy. The government tried to cool the jets recently by limiting new speculation to two units. Sales dipped, but only slightly, and then took off again, pulling along developers eager to add capacity. There's too much capacity now, and sooner or later, it will correct.

Looking at China's wildly inefficient capital allocation, and knowing they aren't idiots, it makes you wonder whether the big spend on real estate isn't about anything real at all.

Bump Two: The Limits of Steroid Stimulus

Here's a simple question you should ask your friends: What's the largest driver in the Chinese economy? When I ask it, the answer is usually either a version of "manufacturing" or "exports." Wrong and wrong. It's investment itself. Fixed-asset investments account for more than 60 percent of China's economic activity. Some of that, roughly 25 percent, is pure real estate transactions as you read earlier, which still puts a whole lot of yuan on the jobsite and in the supply chain, stretching all the way back to the mines, the coal fields, and the steel mills. Globally, those industries—from construction to steelmaking—have all integrated advanced technologies that make them more efficient, more productive, and cleaner. In China, not so much.

Bamboo scaffolding is used in all but China's tallest buildings; it requires more workers to assemble and can't hold the same weight, so moving materials takes longer and requires even more workers. The Chinese steel and copper industries are made up of thousands of small and mid-sized mills and smelters that use more workers to produce less metal at lower quality than the modern technologies can. Copper- and steel-makers in China are poster children for industry consolidation, but the Chinese bosses have resisted.

An acquaintance that was in China recently brought back stories of huge construction crews—hundreds of men—breaking concrete with sledgehammers and digging building-sized foundations with shovels, even as jackhammers and front-end loaders were visible on the site. She also told the story of seeing a crew of workers whose job description seemed to consist of nothing more than scraping stickers and gum off of Beijing's streets and walls. Somebody's gotta do it, right? She says later that day she also saw another crew that seemed to be doing nothing more than putting stickers on the streets and walls. Even if we're completely wrong on translating that one, there's a lot of inefficiency in the Chinese system. Why?

China's market reforms fired the starting gun on an unprecedented human migration. In just a few decades, 130 million people have migrated from the countryside to the cities, making it the largest human migration on record. And those are mostly voluntary. It's the recent involuntary migrations that are especially worrisome. One and a half million people were forced out of their homes and farms to make room for the Three Gorges Dam. Throughout the 1990s, the government moved farmers and fishermen into cities hundreds or thousands of miles away. It didn't go well. A majority of the resettled people have left the cities, and returned—often illegally—to their home regions. And the dam itself? A disaster in almost every way but one.

The Yangtze River is among the most silted in the world. As all the muck builds up, the gates that let water flow over the turbines are becoming clogged. The unregulated logging around the river and dam reservoir have stripped the hillsides and sent massive landslides into the already clogged waterways. In fact, because the dam and reservoir have so disrupted the local environment, the government says that a half a million more people are going to have to move. Oh, they're 15 years into the project and it's not finished yet. So how was this thing *not* a disaster? A hundred thousand Chinese were put to work, at least for a few years. Now the Chinese government is preparing for another relocation project, their largest yet, in the central province of Shaanxi, where the mountains are sliding away and the Yangtze needs more room. Nearly three million people will be moved into the cities.

This is China's immigration story, and it's putting enormous pressures on the government to provide jobs for hundreds of millions of people. It's America's depression-era WPA, on steroids. And it's been going on in China for a lot longer than their pseudo capitalist lifestyle. Remember how I mentioned The Great Wall as the world's first global security infrastructure? Let's revisit that in the light of what we know about China's capital allocation: After all, the thing took 300 years to build, plenty of time for the Mongols to find an alternate route. The Great Wall, it seems, was mostly a great employment project.

Somewhere, deep in the accounting offices of China's central government, smart people are looking at these inefficiencies and saying "This is nuts." They probably know enough to keep their mouths shut. "Until everyone admits the Emperor is naked," they think, "we'll keep complimenting him on the economic miracle fabric he's wrapped himself in."

Talk about exposed.

Capital markets reward efficiency and punish inefficiency. So far, China's low-cost labor advantage has made up the difference. But for how long? A first-year economics major can tell you that systemic inefficiencies are either corrected by markets, or the system itself collapses. The first is wrenching; the second is disastrous.

Bump Three: Kids Today

As you've noticed by now, I love demographics. They set the foundation for all the economic activity that is so often seen as the whole picture, when really it's just the trailing indicator of deeply embedded demographic realities. And the demographer in me just can't get enough of China's one-child policy. That was another of Deng Xiaoping reforms and in 1978 it made sense. Deng and his people knew that China's population was getting ahead of the country's ability to feed, house, and treat them medically. That policy also brought mobility to the labor market with more parents able to move to the cities and work because they weren't raising five kids on the farm. More workers with fewer dependents meant more money for saving and spending. It also positioned China as the place where labor was plentiful and cheap. Perfect timing once again as the American Baby Boomers roared into their high spending, family-raising years. "Made in China" was making a good name for itself.

Fast-forward twenty years and we're starting to see what happens when demographic certainty meets economic correction.

The sharp drop in global consumer demand that is defining this period in our economic history couldn't come at a worse time for China. Exports are down and labor costs are going up—China's young people, most of them only children, are entering the workforce and realizing just how much they can get for a day's labor. In the heavily industrialized coastal cities, manufacturers compete for workers and workers demand higher wages. In several high-profile manufactures, including Honda's China operation, workers have gone out on strike and come back to fatter pay envelopes. China's young working class has started to see its earning power, and wants some new Nikes, and an iPhone, and everything else kids today want.

Now those low-cost labor advantages aren't so low anymore. China is trying to pivot from a being a working-class nation of low-cost manufacturers to a middle-class nation of high-tech precision manufacturers. Innovation is becoming more important than population and raw labor. Meanwhile, the new Asian tigers of Vietnam, Bangladesh, Thailand, and others are happy to grab some of the low-wage work. If China can't make that pivot—and there are a myriad of reasons why it's proving very difficult, beginning with their s-DNA—they are going to trip over their own Nikes.

Bump Four: Little Emperors and Their Smooth, Soft Hands

More demographics: China's population growth of 0.6 percent is among the lowest in the developing world; the one-child policy worked in that regard. But between 2012 and 2015, China's working-age population will peak as a share of the total. After that, more and more elderly will be relying on fewer and fewer workers. The raw numbers of workers are still large, but so are the aged dependents. By 2050 China will have more people over 60 than America will have people.

Every aging nation shares at least one challenge: old people need more health care and caregivers. Health care is expensive everywhere, and in China the caregivers are soon to be in short supply. It's been called the 4-2-1 Problem. Four grandparents + two parents, with only one son to support them in their old age. This is overly reductive, of course. While approximately 40 percent of China's population *has* been subject to the policy, there are exceptions. Farming families can stock up on kids, and families are now allowed to have more than one child if the first is a girl. Wealthier families can simply pay the fine, while others ignore the policy altogether, and enforcement is uneven. And yet there are millions and millions of families with a single son or grandson.

By the way, you're probably familiar with the Chinese cultural belief that it's better to have a son than a daughter. Confucius got that idea rolling, which means it's locked deep in the Chinese s-DNA.

And the sons themselves? After being the apple of so many peoples' eyes all their lives, some aren't so eager to "eat bitterness" like their parents and grandparents before. It's not fair to call them soft. After all, it's young men who are powering the comparatively small but energized entrepreneurial sector. It's also clear to China watchers that a massive generation of young Chinese men are out to make more than sacrifices; they want to make a good life for themselves. All of which means the Chinese government will have to assume more of the caretaking for the aging population.

Bump Five: The Rise of Middle-Class Militants and the Fall of Single-Party Politics

This is a huge bump, and it's harder to gauge accurately, in part because it should have already happened. The contradictions in China's operating system, i.e., communists as capitalists, are infinitely more complex and conflicted than they already sound.

Although the communist government has maintained a tight grip on the political system and free speech, the economy is largely in the hands of autonomous, well-connected industrialists who might make America's old robber barons blush. Corruption is legendary and government officials, especially the farther you are from Beijing, can be seen as nothing more than a security service for the industries that pay them in thick red envelopes. This works well enough when it doesn't have to work too hard—when labor is cheap and big orders are arriving all day long. But as you read earlier, China's industries that gorged on the low-hanging fruit need to climb a little higher in the tree; they need to innovate, take some smart risks, and make some big plays.

Unfortunately for them, the Communist Party they fed is now too fat to climb anything. China's bloated and bureaucratic communist government presents more obstacles than answers. It happened in Russia; it happened in Japan. Single-party politics don't work when business gets tough. The next generation of Chinese business leaders needs a strategic partner in their government officials. Counter intuitively, that also means *more* regulation from the government. What business gets now is a government firing squad to dispatch the plant manager who adds rat poison to the baby formula just so he can make his monthly number. Everybody takes that hit: consumer confidence falls inside China, and exports plunge.

Perhaps more than anything, China's business sector needs a government that's not obsessed with its citizens' Google searches and blog posts, or baffled by how to respond to a middle class that they helped create.

The communists sure as hell know how to rule over poor people, and they understand that keeping the rich happy is essentially about keeping the poor in line and off the streets. The middle class? These people own a big part of China's recent success. They are educated and accomplished. They went in big on the dreams their government was selling. And most importantly, they are *not* little children and they won't be ruled that way indefinitely.

Bump Six: Social Unrest, Meet Social Malaise

Here's one that's even deeper under the Chinese skin, and thus difficult for Americans like me to decode. Here's what I see: In 2009 the British medical journal, *The Lancet*, published the results of a World Health Organization-funded study on mental illness in China. Over 60,000 adults were interviewed, and some startling facts emerged. According to the study, 17 percent, or more than one in five adults, have a mental illness as defined by the DSM—the Diagnostic and Statistical Manual of Mental Disorders, which sets the de-facto global standards for diagnosis. The study also revealed that fewer than one in twenty adults ever seek professional care. That's not surprising given the shame-based Chinese culture, but this might surprise you: The leading cause of death among people fifteen to thirty-four is suicide. Here's another: China is the only nation in the world where women kill themselves at higher rates than men. In rural areas the most popular method is drinking pesticide, which results in an agonizing and horrific death. In urban areas they jump from buildings and bridges, prompting some companies and local governments to install "suicide nets."

Something isn't working here. Let's dig deeper.

Peoples' problems in China are sometimes separated into two realms: household issues, which include the private dynamics of families and marriages; and national issues, or politics, essentially. People are culturally encouraged to leave those problems to the government and keep any doubts to themselves. I wonder if those two realms overlap and feed each other in contemporary China. It could be that the Chinese s-DNA is in turmoil as China's political leaders lead the people into a very non-Confucian future.

Family is at the core of the Confucian ideal, and families are splintered with every young person's departure for the city. The cities have also nurtured an affluent class that divides the nation in a different way, equally as disruptive. Competition in the cities is beyond brutal, and hundreds of local colleges have opened with the promise of giving students an edge. Families can easily drain their life's savings so that a son (or daughter) can attain a degree, which practically guarantees they are in the city for good. And all just for money.

Maybe capitalism at all costs has actually cost the Chinese something they weren't prepared to pay. In America, we hear a lot of family-first rhetoric, but leaving home often means not really looking back. Heck, good parents in my neighborhood are the ones who best *prepared* the kids for independence. And as Americans we've never been subjected to the same kind of narrow-bore government-issued dream that the Chinese have. We expect to have choices and we make them. They're not always right, or always 100 percent our own, but only the most pathetic will claim they were cheated.

I wonder if some of the parents and grandparents feel cheated, after devoting their lives to a child who's nowhere to be seen, or if the kid feels cheated after pounding him or herself into the impossible shape of China's ideal. If that's true, I'm pretty sure it's trouble.

Bump Seven: Widespread Environmental Degradation and Overwhelmed Public Health

The 2008 Summer Olympics in Beijing introduced the world to China's horrendous air quality. China is the world's biggest CO^2 emitter and it shows in every urban area: buildings shrouded in haze, noses and mouths covered by masks. What we *can't* see right away looks equally murky: water.

According to a 2008 World Health Organization report, roughly 100 million Chinese do not have access to a reliably clean water supply. Over 450 million—more than the entire U.S. population—don't have access to modern sanitation. Only 20 percent of Chinese wastewater is treated; in developed countries the average is 80 percent. Seventy-five percent of Chinese lakes are unsafe, and that's the water supply for nearly all the major Chinese cities.

It's a public health nightmare.

Infectious diseases are common killers in China. The SARS epidemic started here; tuberculosis and its virulent offspring MDR-TB (multi-drug-resistant tuberculosis) are widespread. In rural areas, the close contact between people and animals makes for a viral melting pot that would challenge even the best public health systems; Chinese villages have small clinics—maybe. Of course microbial enemies have been part of the human experience for all time. Now, along with modernity, the so-called lifestyle diseases are crashing the Chinese party. Diabetes and heart disease. Lung cancer. Hypertension. Obesity. Chinese citizens are dying from chronic, non-communicable diseases at alarming rates—80 percent of total deaths, according to *International Journal of Epidemiology*.

It's scary to guess how bad it might get for the population. Right now, it's bad enough for the economy: The World Bank estimated that, "environmental degradation and subsequent public health problems have the potential to take 8 to 12 percent off China's $5 trillion GDP."

Bump Eight: Let Them Eat Coal

Environmental hazards stem from what industry spits out. What they take in is just as frightening. China is the world's number one importer of iron ore. They dig up a lot of coal and they import even more. Saudi Arabia sells more oil to China than it does to the U.S. China imports almost all of its high-grade finished copper. (As you read earlier, Chinese copper smelters aren't up to spec.) As recently as a few years ago, China was both the world's number one steel producer *and* the world's number one steel importer. Taken together, it's demand such as the world has never witnessed. China is hungry for resources, and they're hungry, period.

The warming planet has dried out the once-productive field in China's south. Five billion tons of fertile soil is lost to erosion annually, and silt discharge from the Yangtze River exceeds the Nile and Amazon combined. All this is happening just as urbanized Chinese people have developed an appetite for steak, fine chesses, and a tall glass of milk. Cattle operations require huge amounts of clean water, which in China today is not only polluted but has never been in great supply—Chinese territories have just roughly seven percent of the world's fresh water supply. (And about one-fifth of the world's people, who get thirsty just like cows.) Remember the earlier stat about China making *and* importing the most steel? It's true for dairy products too: they make more, and import more, than any other nation. Amazing.

As authorities scramble to increase agricultural production, they're also hedging their bets. China has been buying or leasing enormous amounts of farmland in South America and Africa. Some of those areas are already dealing with food scarcity and the accompanying high prices. But how long will hungry people move peacefully off the road so that trucks filled with Chinese-purchased wheat can pass?

China's diplomatic policy is often described as "soft power." Instead of sending in soldiers to protect their interests or to respond to a humanitarian crisis, they wait for things to settle down and then arrive with those fat red envelopes. China is the only nation with oil contracts with both Iraqi Kurds and Iraqi Arabs. In Afghanistan they're putting $3 billion dollars in a copper mine.

We get it. Geo-politics is first and foremost about taking care of your own people. And as we're well aware, global resources like food, oil, and water are finite. Scarcity and risk can be priced. Panic, however, cannot—not even for all the money in China.

THE LONG ROAD OF NATIONS

Please forgive my strident tone. I don't mean to alarm, just inform. The Chinese success story papers over serious cracks, and potentially huge obstacles loom that can derail their progress. That progress, such as it is, has had Americans bamboozled for a decade, and lately we seem to be completely freaked out. But instead of watching China and trying to figure out their formula, I suggest that China take a closer look at the American story. We've been riding the capitalist road for a couple hundred years and we've ridden across some of the biggest bumps in history. Not only did we survive, but we got stronger.

Five

Tenacity in the Tank: The U.S. Then, Now, and in the Future

The bumps ahead in China's capitalist road trip are uniquely their own. Their nation will be challenged by the communist/capitalist operating system they've assembled, and by factors related to the source code underneath it—their own s-DNA. Here in the West, we should all be rooting for them. If your inborn American competitiveness resists cheering them on, at least hope that the worst can be avoided. In subsequent chapters we'll explore why. In this chapter, I aim to remind readers of how the U.S. has been tested and torn by bumps that were, like China's now, uniquely our own.

To American and Western readers, our own bumps are object lessons in the hazards of free markets and even freedom itself. But there's the bathwater, and then there's the baby. The baby stays. The bumps are not critical commentaries on the systems of capitalism or democracy. Rather, they are clear-eyed assessments of what can go wrong within them. Good ideas on very bad days, if you will.

The Civil War, the bank panics and stock market crashes, and the Great Depression each have generated libraries of historical records and commentaries. An un-tenured, part-time economic historian like me isn't going to add much those shelves. Where I can, perhaps, provide some new information and even insight to readers of *Tenacious* is in what happened next: What were the economic outcomes of the aftermaths, and how were they driven by expressions of American s-DNA? In every case, something essential in the American character was called into question, if not assaulted outright. And in every case, it was that same American character that emerged stronger because of it. As it happens, business picked up, too.

THE CIVIL WAR

By American standards, nothing destroyed as much or as many, or penetrated the nation's soul as violently as the Civil War. Six hundred and twenty thousand or more were killed and over 400,000 were wounded in just under four bloody years. The U.S. lost 2 percent of its population, the equivalent of over six million Americans today. The Union army paid a higher price in human lives, but in purely commercial terms, the Confederate states absorbed the greatest losses.

Much of the fighting took place on Southern soil. Farms and crops were decimated. Countless homes and businesses were destroyed. Emancipation of the slaves erased the Southern landholders' largest capital investment; slaves were more valuable than even the land they plowed. Confederate bonds and currency were worthless and the banking system was almost totally destroyed. The South was left with virtually no capital, and extremely limited means to generate it. A quarter of Southern men between the ages of twenty and forty died. The Union had been preserved, but the defeated states of the South were decades away from contributing much to the recovering nation.

In the North, the picture is more complex. War economies can create opportunities and accelerate some industries; they can also disrupt broad economic drivers like interest rates, monetary policy, labor markets, and more.

The largest Northern industry was built on the *South's* chief agricultural product: cotton. With their supply suddenly cut to near zero, numerous cotton textile mills folded. Some also converted to wool, which doubled in production output during the war. American innovators responded with a flurry of inventions and process improvements. Soldiers needed uniforms, and sewing machines went from rare and expensive to common and economical, and their machine-made interchangeable parts would become a model for other industries. Borden's condensed milk was introduced and quickly became a key calorie source for the Union soldiers. The absence of men in the fields created an opening for advancement in labor-saving farm implements.

At the same time, there were significant negatives. Inflation rose steadily, challenging the viability of a national paper currency, which was first issued broadly during the war to replace the notes issued by local banks and businesses that, once out of town, had no value. Confidence in the new U.S. "greenbacks" wasn't much better, and inflation soared. By the war's end, the cost of living was 75 percent higher than in 1860, and wholesale prices peaked at double their prewar levels. New trade unions arose and gained power during the war as labor shortages empowered workers. One of the consistent engines of manpower stopped chugging along, too—European immigrants stayed home, understanding that the first thing they were likely to hear upon landing in the U.S. was "Welcome to America. This way to the battle." Indeed, many fought and many died. Many more watched from an ocean away.

As the enthusiastic predictions of a quick Union victory met the reality of a long and costly war, new investments slowed and Northern industries settled in for a long, grinding conflict. In 1862, the *New York Tribune* groused about "our paralyzed industry." But let's be clear. The trauma of the Civil War was felt most deeply not in the wallets of Americans, but in their hearts. And no single American felt the trauma more deeply, or embodied it more completely than Abraham Lincoln.

It's true that the first Republican president opposed slavery, but like so many things with Lincoln, it's not that simple. He expressed doubts about African-Americans' ability to take responsible roles in a democracy, and he supported the Fugitive Slave Act, which put law enforcement to work capturing runaway slaves, even in free states. As a private attorney, he had represented a slave owner trying to recapture his "property."

Lincoln as president was a strict constitutionalist. He knew full well the hazards of his unconstitutional acts. Lincoln suspended the constitutional right of habeas corpus and implemented a virtual martial law in some regions. He instituted a military draft, which led to violent riots in New York and elsewhere. For some time he remained deeply conflicted about slavery, but not about the Union. In a letter to Horace Greeley, he wrote

> *If I could save the Union without freeing any slave I would do it, and if I could save it by freeing all the slaves I would do it; and if I could save it by freeing some and leaving others alone I would also do that.*

As the war slogged on toward its conclusion, Lincoln's moral clarity sharpened—not only in regard to the slaves but also the white Southerners. He would entertain no armistice proposal that allowed the bondage of blacks to continue, but he refused to cast blame for the war or to express any moral righteousness. After all, it was the American founders who made slavery legal, not Southern plantation owners. Lincoln wanted reconciliation with the South, not their humiliation. In his second inaugural address, that much is clear:

> *With malice toward none, with charity for all, with firmness in the right as God gives us to see the right, let us strive on to finish the work we are in, to bind up the nation's wounds, to care for him who shall have borne the battle and for his widow and his orphan, to do all which may achieve and cherish a just and lasting peace among ourselves and with all nations.*

Unfortunately, with Lincoln dead, the Reconstruction of the South included plenty of malice. It was brutal on Southern whites and freed slaves alike. There *was* humiliation, and there *was* bondage, now in the form of sharecropping. Whites disenfranchised blacks, and the North disenfranchised the entire region. In another nation, the war and its aftermath might well have sown seeds of resentment and violence that would fester over the generations, and then erupt in violence. In some corners of the South resentment endures, but the states are united because the American s-DNA is resilient. Carrying a grudge can drag a person down, or worse—I've always liked this quote by Augustine of Hippo: "Resentment is like taking poison and hoping the other person dies."

After the war, the nation of immigrants saw immigrants return. The transcontinental railroad was completed. Several laws that had been passed during the war were acted upon with great eagerness. The Land Grant colleges were established. The Homestead Act said to anyone, American or immigrant, Northern or Southern, "There's 160 acres out West for you and your family. Stay on it five years, and it's yours, *and* you're an American citizen."

In other words, Americans picked up the Industrial Revolution right where we left off, and got busy again building America. A hundred and fifty years after The Civil War, we haven't stopped examining what it meant and how it's carried forward. I offer this modest assessment: A true and terrifying darkness fell on America, and we brought ourselves through it because of who we are. And who we are hasn't changed.

TRUST-BUSTING AND THE PANIC OF 1907

Teddy Roosevelt took office in 1901 when an assassin's bullet killed William McKinley. Soon after, it was Roosevelt himself doing the firing. In his sights were the behemoths that were trampling American ideals—the political machines, the corrupt unions, and more than anything else, the trusts. Roosevelt was a rich man who never lost touch with, or affection for, the hard-working everyday American. He saw our s-DNA as it was accumulating, and he was a warrior for what it represented in the early years of the new century.

Roosevelt went after J.D. Rockefeller's Standard Oil, a monopoly by any measure, and broke it into separate companies that had to actually compete for business. In a bruising battle with John Pierpont Morgan, Roosevelt brought regulations and merchant protections to the railroads. And with so many things about the man, his reputation as a "trust buster" has been simplified to support the mythology; the facts are more nuanced and truer to the core principles of capitalism. Roosevelt sought to regulate rather than dissolve most trusts outright. He worked to find a balance between the reach of government, the rights of laborers, and the interests of business owners.

Then, in October of 1907, it all quickly fell apart.

After a speculator's big play to corner the copper market failed miserably, an out-sized panic spread across America's banking system. Bank runs quickly brought the entire financial sector to near collapse. There was no central bank, no Federal Reserve, so there were no government structures that could provide immediate liquidity and calm. We didn't really have a mommy to run too, but we did have J.P. Morgan.

The banker and trust baron who had gone toe-to-toe with Roosevelt and the new U.S. regulatory systems stepped into the breach not once, but twice. First, Morgan put his fortune on the line as a guarantee to New York depositors, and urged other bankers to follow his lead. Over the course of two tense weeks and with Morgan as the most trusted adult in the room, the panic was downgraded to mere anxiety. Then we took another hit.

In November, the Tennessee Coal, Iron and Railroad Company (TCI) teetered on the brink of ruin thanks to the imminent bankruptcy of a brokerage firm that had borrowed heavily to invest in TCI. A failure of the brokerage firm, or of TCI, would severely damage the nation's shaky confidence. J.P. Morgan moved in once again, playing both mommy and mogul. He offered to buy the brokerage and assume control of TCI. The problem was that Morgan also controlled U.S. Steel, and absorbing TCI would put him back on the wrong side of Roosevelt's anti-trust cops. In this case, liquidity and market confidence mattered more to Roosevelt than handcuffing the monopolists. He approved the deal and exempted U.S. Steel from any anti-trust violations. The recovery was back on track.

Roosevelt's critics howled and called him a hypocrite. After leaving office, the government even tried (but failed) to reverse the merger. For all his everyman progressive ideals, Roosevelt understood that American business also needed big industries and big ambitions like J.P. Morgan's. It wasn't always tidy, and it was rarely heroic, but Teddy was an able steward of the evolving American s-DNA. We are principled, *and* we are practical. Encouraged by the newly created Federal Reserve, we got back on the bike and roared into the 1920s.

THE CRASH OF 1929 AND THE GREAT DEPRESSION

The Civil War will probably always be the dark night of America's soul. The 1929 Crash and the Great Depression that followed drained something vital from America's dreams. These dual calamities were, and remain, the most severe tests that American capitalism has confronted. We got punched in the face, or rather we punched ourselves in the face. Then we were beaten down repeatedly in a dusty and disheartening decade.

In the years leading up to the 1929 Crash, America was throwing a hell of a party. It was at once a Gilded Age do-over and a bawdy night in a speakeasy. And why not celebrate? The U.S. had just been instrumental in bringing WWI to a close without much loss of American life, at least compared to the European combatants. And in doing so, we also moved up a couple of geo-political weight classes. We had swagger—not just militarily, but economically too.

World War I fundamentally altered America's economic relationship with Europe. We were now not only their ally or a former enemy; we were also their banker. American banks financed much of Europe's reconstruction, which also included selling to them the products of American industry. They borrowed American capital to buy American imports. That was destined to end badly.

Here at home, encouraged by everyone from President Hoover on down, millions of regular people were hopping into the bull market for the first time. Thanks to rising wages, folks had more money in their pockets, and relaxed underwriting standards meant banks were happy to stuff in a little more. Stocks were paying fat dividends and companies sure looked profitable. Margin buying became widespread, which put house money in the hands of rookie investors. Fundamentals were for fuddy-duddies, and the wild volatility was just part of the crazy fun. That was September of 1929.

By mid October, the fun was gone and big crazy was threatening. Those companies Americans all owned together were worth nowhere near their stock prices, and the bull couldn't hide them anymore. Sell orders flooded in on October 24, Black Thursday. That eternal grown-up, J.P. Morgan tried to calm the markets again, buying up millions of shares and bringing some stability to the markets by Friday. But the weekend was full of worried chatter, and Monday's opening bell brought only fevered selling. By Tuesday, Black Tuesday, the panic was on. Wall Street had crashed. It was the most devastating day in American financial history. In the few weeks that followed, thirty billion dollars vanished from the U.S. economy.

Tenacity in the Tank

Of course, not everybody had played the game. There were still millions of Americans whose individual balance sheets didn't look any worse after the crash. But everyone felt scared, and behaved that way. Banks failed as withdrawals zeroed out their vaults. Business owners who had re-invested profits in stocks were ruined. Factories were shuttered overnight, and 100,000 businesses were gone by 1932. Unemployment was as devastating as it was sudden. Two-income families were rare, so when the factory where dad worked closed, the whole family was in crisis. Many families disintegrated into homelessness and the hobo entered the American lexicon. Foreclosed homeowners weren't paying property taxes either, which meant local governments were just as broke as their residents.

We had crashed the bike hard and left it mangled on the side of the road. In 1932, we walked into the voting booth and tossed Mommy-in-chief Herbert Hoover on his ear. Americans were ready for a new parent with a New Deal.

Franklin D. Roosevelt's New Deal has returned to the conversation here in late 2011 as the current administration wrestles with some of the same challenges Roosevelt did. What should government do when business isn't hiring? When does the social safety net begin to strangle initiative? Is the government in the lead, or in the way? The right answers aren't any clearer now than they were then.

Conservative economists of the day were convinced that the Great Depression was a painful but necessary correction—America didn't need a new deal or more government, it just needed more time and less regulation. Liberal thinkers argued that capitalism needed a government that was responsive to the social needs of the people. The hard-core leftists, and there were many, argued that market capitalism had failed and the government must assert itself more strongly.

History shows us which mommy we ran toward, not pure leftist, but left of center for sure. Roosevelt's New Deal programs began to take shape in the form of new dams and rural electrification projects in seven southern states (the TVA) and new parks and roads built by eight million unemployed breadwinners (the WPA). Several Federal agencies were born under the New Deal: Social Security, the FDIC, and the Securities and Exchange Commission. An entirely new species of mother had been assembled, and before she could get us all the way back on the bike, the Japanese interrupted the healing. No—actually they accelerated it.

The industrial demands of building the war machine did wonders for the nation's employers, and the shared fury over Pearl Harbor united the country in ways New Deal policies never could. We kept Roosevelt in the president's chair longer than we expected and we let his replacement, Harry Truman, finish the job. At that point, our need for any help from mom was long over. Dwight Eisenhower was the new man for the job, and Ike was no one's mommy.

The following chart tells a remarkable story about American resilience. We don't just get back to normal after an internal crisis or worldwide upheaval; we grow stronger than ever.

Look at the Dow after WWI: up 300 points. After WWII, up 800, and after Vietnam, up 9,000. Maybe we actually need a good 'ole global crisis every generation or so.

The Bounce in Our Dips

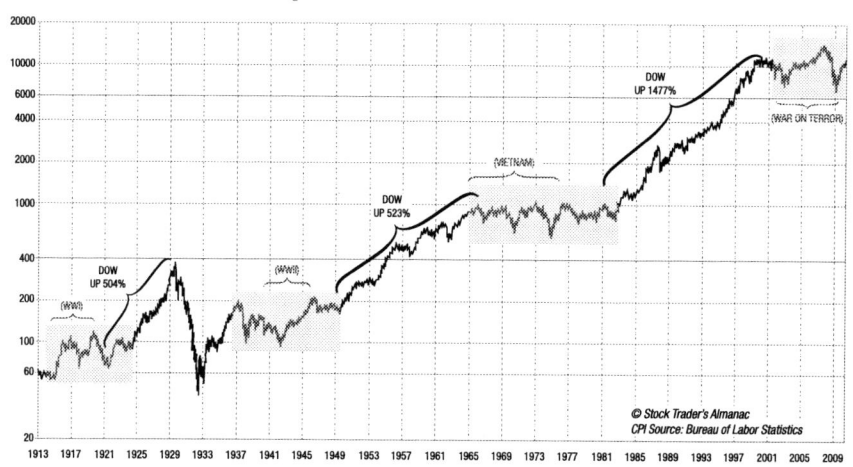

THE AMERICAN SECRET SAUCE

In that whirlwind tour of American bounce-back, I hope you saw something besides economics: politics. I believe that the American political system, as tortured and paralyzed as it can seem at times, is a vital source of American tenacity.

I'm nuts, right?

Consider this: With every major upheaval in American's economic system, we move a little to the political left, where the hands-on government ethos is used to repair the damage. If the damage is deep, the repair is more systemic, i.e., the Glass-Steagall Act, or the new agencies of the New Deal. We ran to Roosevelt and then got busy making babies after the war. "The stock market crash? I heard my grandpa talking about that. . ."

If the damage is on the surface, then the repairs are, too. The S&L Crisis of the late 1980s and early 1990s was a crisis in name only. Nevertheless, there was a small tumble and as we were assessing the damage, we handed the keys to Bill Clinton. Even if John McCain had been a better candidate, the Financial Crisis of 2008 cast the deciding vote and elected Barack Obama.

If it looks like I'm talking politics, I'm not. I'm illustrating the dynamic nature of our political system. Democracy is the secret sauce we've been making in the underground kitchen of American s-DNA. It's the system we invented when we went from colonists to revolutionaries to founding fathers and families. And it's the system we continue to build now as our need for shelter shifts with the kind of weather we're having.

Politics are ugly up close. It dithers and postures and embarrasses us all. Some days the best we can hope for is entertainment. I say take the long view. Look back at our history and see what we did, or didn't do, to get better after we got hurt. Our political system doesn't respond in real time—and that's a good thing—but it does respond. We get the government we need at the time, and then we get back on the bike stronger than we were before.

Let's circle back quickly to China, and think again about the government they've created. The one-party system, and an authoritarian one at that, sure can truncate debate and deliver everybody to a policy quickly. If China has shown us anything, it's that they can execute a plan (among other things). Yet execution in all forms has its limitations; flexibility and responsiveness matter less than hierarchy and obedience. China believes they have the right recipe, or at least they're acting like they do. Unfortunately, a lot of Americans now are buying it too. In the next chapter, we'll unpack some of those Made in China assumptions and see just how durable they are.

Six

Innovators, Imitators, and Immigrants: Challenging Assumptions

Another strong current, or rather several of them, flow directly into American anxiety about China. These currents move below the frenetic day-to-day news cycle or even the wider rhythms of normal business cycles. In the minds of many people, these currents have cut such deep grooves that they're on par with rigorously validated scientific facts. The truth is, they are assumptions. And in this chapter we're going to do more than question them; we're going to drain some of the force from their stubborn persistence.

A number of my arguments against the received wisdom are based in the deep s-DNA of both Americans and Chinese. Others are closer to the surface and use macroeconomics to make the point. That said, we're out to do more than merely bust a few myths. My intent is to help readers assemble something new with the pieces and parts of broken assumptions—I believe we're heading into a new Renaissance, with America's s-DNA driving it toward global prosperity. But I'm getting ahead of myself. Let's crack open a few knuckleheaded beliefs.

BELIEF: AMERICA DOESN'T MAKE ANYTHING ANYMORE

This belief is often exhibit A in the argument for China's continued ascendency: "The economy that makes nothing and only consumes is weak and dependent." It's wrong in many ways, beginning with the absolute of "nothing."

The United States' annual manufacturing output is somewhere between $1.5 trillion to $2.15 trillion, depending on how you slice the data. Leave *out* mining and utilities, and we're at the low number; keep them *in*, and that's the higher figure. Now, let's compare outputs.

Not only does the U.S. still make stuff, we make twice as much as Japan, four times as much as Germany, and roughly 45 percent more than China. China's reporting to the rest of the world is limited, but

Manufacturing output of the top eight manufacturing nations
(Includes mining and utilities)

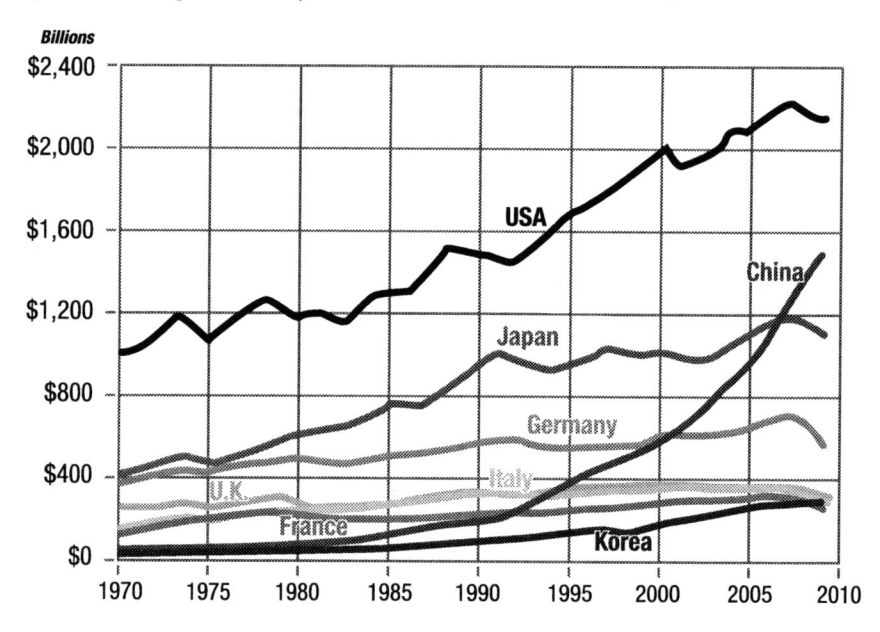

Source: United Nations, http://unstats.un.org/unsd/snaama/dnllist.asp

Innovators, Imitators, and Immigrants

their reports to the United Nation are viewed as the most reliable, and always include mining and utility data. Even if you wanted to handicap the comparison by removing mining and utilities from the U.S. output (as is typically the case) the U.S. still manufactures more than any other nation.

There's another revealing insight on the previous chart. Look at how the lines zigzag up and down for the U.S., Japan, and Germany. That's the market responding to fluctuations in demand—less demand means less output, more demand means more. It's the happy story of a healthy demand economy. Now look at China; a nice smooth line and a violation of the accepted economic laws. That's because there is relatively little classic economic demand in the Chinese economy. China is a command economy. They're spending a lot of money in ways that simply don't make good economic sense. They're building infrastructure no one needs; there's no demand for it. Chinese officials command a new mall, or highway, or dam, and it kick-starts all kinds of spending that acts like rocket fuel to their output metrics. Capitalist economies have foolish spending too, and some of ours originates in Washington D.C. But our own pork-filled federal budgets and legislative earmarks would hardly be noticed compared to the spending (and buying) that happens every quarter in today's China.

Yet, demand or command is a distinction that doesn't mean much when Americans make a quick trip to Target. It's rare to flip over a label or look at the packaging on a toy or electronics product and *not* see "Made in China." What looks like a disaster to the American economy is really economics as usual. China is really just the latest of low-cost manufacturers who have made their name in low-wage, low-margin manufacturing sectors. Remember "Made in Hong Kong"? Or "Made in Taiwan"? For years, toys, apparel, consumer electronics, and a lot of other goods that fill American stores have been manufactured outside our borders, often in an Asian country. China is so visible in the aisles Americans travel every day because China has managed to "out Asia" Asia. And it won't continue.

As you read earlier, Chinese manufacturers are competing for low-cost labor. That's good news for the laborers themselves. Wages are rising, nearly 12 percent a year in some reports. Labor is still cheap by most standards, especially American, since the average manufacturing wage in China is still only $3.10 an hour; in the U.S. it's $22.30. And yet, in China's five largest manufacturing provinces, the Chinese government has raised the minimum wage 14 percent to 21 percent in the past year. That's good news for Chinese workers, and for Chinese officials who want to manage social unrest. It's bad news for thousands of low-end, labor-intensive, export-oriented manufacturers.

For 30 years, China has sold its labor cheap and paid its actual laborers even less. All along the way, they've been pocketing the difference. Now they're spending it, and looking rich, but labor's costing more. China is already losing its competitiveness in apparel, shoes, electronics, and other products as countries like Vietnam grab larger and larger shares.

Take that trend all the way out and you can almost hear the middle-class Shanghai manager sighing, as he looks through the labels in his family's closet, "China doesn't make anything anymore."

BELIEF: ONLY MANUFACTURING ECONOMIES ARE SUCCESSFUL ECONOMIES

This is one that's been dying a slow death for a long, long time. The craftsmen who made three tables a year said it when technology turned "makers" into "assemblers." The unions say it when they propose their labor-centric solutions for the country, and the politicians say it when they are standing on a factory floor shaking hands for votes. If we lose our manufacturing chops—whether it's mastery of handsaws or raw employment numbers—we lose our advantage. Everyone says it, or so it seems. To my contrarian sensibilities that also means it's probably wrong.

I hold that it's a fallacy to believe in manufacturing as the sole determinant of economic health. Does manufacturing add value to an economy? Absolutely, but only some of it. In fact, in most manufacturing sectors there's more downside risk than there is upside reward. Take the two largest inputs: material and labor.

Manufacturing is inherently material intensive. The material could be iron ore or transmission parts. Either way, if they aren't available the lines are impacted. We saw it most vividly in the 2011 Miyagi earthquake and tsunami in Japan. The true economic costs won't stop adding up for several years. But this much is clear: the short-term economic loss was greatest in Japan's manufacturing sector, primarily their electronics and automotive industries. In other words, the dual suns in Japan's economic sky. Plants closed for lack of parts, first in Japan and then across the respective global networks. Of course, there will be plenty of pain to go around—lost wages for many and higher prices for many more. Japan will recover and production will (probably) return to pre-earthquake levels. The rebuilding alone will mean more economic activity in the short term, but not more long-term value. Some of that may be gone forever as supply chains adapt and bad news calls for better thinking.

I'll admit that's a worst-case scenario for manufacturing's inherent resource vulnerability. But look around the world. Do you see climate change and energy scarcities as neutral influences for manufacturing economies? No way. And even when the global supply of raw materials is *theoretically* adequate that doesn't mean the prices are going to stay predictable. Fierce global demands and pre-emptive supply manipulations are going to mean volatility rules. Commodities have never been the most logical of economics, and they're on their way to becoming even nuttier. And again, the overall costs will ultimately be spread wide, but how many manufacturers will fail along the way simply because they couldn't afford to ride the swings?

On the labor side of the equation, the movement in costs is less volatile, but people aren't.

There's limit to how little a factory owner can pay a person for an hour of work, or how many hours they can get from them. When wages remain low and hours stay long, the manager had better hope there's a line of people outside ready to take the next job, When there's not, costs are going to rise. It's a pure supply-and-demand argument, and if you're a manufacturer making margins of pennies or less just to compete, how much room do you have to move? This hard reality—in the U.S., China, or anywhere—makes manufacturing in and of itself a risky space to play in. And if there's a less risky corner of the manufacturing cage match, it's where the West already has an advantage: technology.

Inexpensive labor is inherently low-skilled labor—it's a lot of people doing very simple operations, over and over and over. True leaps in productivity are technology based. It's what made the Industrial Revolution an actual revolution, and it really hasn't stopped since. Manufacturing has long been moving from a labor-driven operation to a technology-driven one. Japan and Germany have baked this into their economies, same with the U.S. And all we had to give up was the jobs. . .

Take another look at the manufacturing output chart earlier in the chapter. The most impressive figure to me is not the raw American output; it's how few Americans were required to get it done. Approximately 12 million Americans show up for work on factory floors. In China, it's 100 million people. Not only are American manufacturers getting more from fewer people, were doing it better than any other nation. In the last year stats were available, productivity in U.S. manufacturing increased by 7.7 percent. According to the Bureau of Labor Statistics, that's a larger gain than advanced manufacturing heavyweights like Germany, Japan, Korea, or Sweden.

And the jobs? They're different now.

Without a doubt, these tech-driven productivity gains have implications for American workers. For generations, Americans equated manufacturing success with job creation. Today, we're seeing these two de-link. Automated manufacturing processes are shrinking labor's share of overall employment, especially poorly skilled and even mid-level skilled workers. American manufacturers are becoming more competitive in the higher margin levels precisely because they've moved beyond the limits of what a worker can lift, and have leveraged the impact of what a worker can invent. It's called innovation, and there are a lot of myths around that, too.

BELIEF: CHINA IS BEATING US IN OUR OWN GAME OF INNOVATION

This one is just irrational fear. Emphasis: *irrational*.

Innovation can only happen with innovators—people who see problems differently, have a high tolerance for instructive failures, and possess the courage to stand up and say "Here's an idea than might work better." It's messy and it's risky. That must be why Americans like it so much.

Ben Franklin, Thomas Edison, Samuel Morse, Alexander Graham Bell, Jonas Salk, the Wright Brothers. They are the heroes in American economic and cultural history; we revere them, we teach their ideas in school; we dream of matching their accomplishments. . .and if we can't do it, maybe our kids will, or their kids. Ingenuity and invention are encoded within the American s-DNA. That alone doesn't make any single American an inventor, but it does make America a place where the inventor's path in all of its messiness is revered.

The failed inventor in the U.S. risks, perhaps, his or her reputation and probably livelihood. No small things. Yet, in China, the failed inventor risks all that and more, sometimes even his or her life.

Innovation is, by definition, a significant improvement in the current norm. Before you can invent the solution you have to identify the problem, and that's the first rub against the Chinese s-DNA. It's hard to remain loyal to your elders and authority when you're being critical of their ideas. Yet there are always iconoclasts, even in China, so let's stay with the scenario and imagine that an idea was so brilliant that its force could not be suppressed. Our young Chinese inventor had a big win, which means *everyone* in the organization is going to take the credit. Sure, there may be a bonus in the pay envelope next week, or maybe not. The individual reward will probably never be larger than that. Still, it beats the alternative.

Imagine the outcome if the big idea turned out to be less than promised. Or, even more likely, it was a good idea that never had the chance to get big in a system that's pushing downward on change. Now our Chinese iconoclast has not only exposed him or herself to shame and ridicule, it's been brought onto the family and maybe the company. Not good. "Now, who's got the next great idea for China? Did I see hand go up? Way in the back? No? Anyone?"

Okay, let's widen the view again, and take in more evidence that China is lagging behind in economic measures of innovation. Before we do, though, see whether you can name a Chinese brand name.

Enduring brands are strongly correlated with innovation. BMW in Germany. Sony, Honda, and Toyota in Japan. Samsung in Korea. The American list could go on for pages. Did you have an answer for the Chinese brand? Most people I ask don't, and the truth is, the Chinese don't do much better because there are no global Chinese brands.

Chinese manufacturers assemble the stuff that top global brands are famous for. Much of Apple's iPhone is made in China. But on a high-end version that costs $300, China is lucky to hold on to $10.

For a pair of Nikes, it's four pennies on the dollar. This focus on low-margin assembly is a tough way to build an economy, but at least it's honest.

In the quest for innovative brands, China is taking counterfeiting to a new level. In late July of 2011, the American business press crackled with the story *not* of counterfeit Apple products, but of entirely counterfeit Apple stores. The big logo, the colorful displays, the contemporary architecture, and of course, loads of fake Apple computers and phones. And the best part? The employees genuinely believed they were Apple employees. That's what they had been told, and besides—there was an Apple logo on their paychecks.

How ironic. Some of the world's most non-traditional retail workers being replicated by some of the world's most tradition-bound people. The story offers more than a punch line, however; it reflects a much larger trend of creative borrowing. Through an initiative called "indigenous innovation," Chinese companies are encouraged to leap forward in high-tech manufacturing by forcing foreign firms into joint ventures that require them to share proprietary processes and product patents if they want to sell their products there. Many western business leaders have called it "intellectual property theft." I call it a cry for help.

China's failure to innovate is the source of great anxiety in that nation. With the low-hanging fruit of simple product manufacturing gone, Chinese manufacturers need to move up the value chain into advanced manufacturing, which requires both precision processes and creative thinking. They'll have to get better in original research, technical development, engineering, and quality control. Not to mention the "soft skills" of market research, market development, and sales. Chinese businesses are filled with executives who have made their careers in small increments of doing what was expected. They know more about placating government officials than they do about understanding customers and building global brands.

If you're still stumped for Chinese brands, let's start with their largest domestic sector, automobiles. There are several Chinese car brands, and they've tried to interest American buyers. They're companies like Brilliance, Geely, Great Wall, and BYD. They've displayed at the big auto shows, and issued promising news releases. The problem is their cars look strangely similar to cars by Mercedes Benz or Chevrolet or Smart or Fiat. Except they don't drive as well, or last as long. It could be a long time before you see a Chinese car behind you at a stoplight, and even longer before one passes you.

BELIEF: CHINA IS OUT-EDUCATING THE U.S., AND DOING A BETTER JOB PREPARING ITS YOUNG PEOPLE TO LEAD THE GLOBAL ECONOMY

First, some context: Americans have never made education a national priority. Neither the Constitution not the Bill of Rights includes the words "education" or "school." In fact, during the two hundred years that bracket the nation's formation—the mid-1600s to mid-1800s—public schools were essentially non-existent. At the same time, several generations of young boys and girls grew into the literate and visionary men and women who would lay the nation's foundation and begin building the country you see today. American public schools didn't make them so smart; America itself did.

In that most important and substantial period, the educational needs of Americans were met by a diverse variety of institutions...homes, churches, and ad-hoc neighborhood schools. Further on the margins were philosophical societies, circulating libraries, and apprenticeships. The first public high school, Boston English High School, didn't open until 1821. Then, it took almost 50 years before we got around to establishing the U.S. Department of Education. That was 1867.

A formalized, rigorous, and compulsory education hasn't been a larger part of the American story simply because Americans haven't valued it more than, well, just about every other ingredient in a successful, fulfilling life. . .hard work, resilience, courage, faith. In other words, we created an educational system that reflects our s-DNA. Does education matter in America? Of course. We've created a university system that attracts millions of students from outside of the U.S., including China. Maybe the more illustrative question is this: Do educational credentials matter in America? In my view, not so much.

One of the questions I like to ask people—and I've asked a lot of people, 500+—is this: One guy is a millionaire who's dropped out of high school; one guy's a millionaire who went to Harvard. Who do you respect more? Americans almost always pick the millionaire dropout. (The exceptions are all Harvard grads, which makes them a teeny bit biased.) When I ask Europeans, roughly 60 percent pick the Harvard grad, and 100 percent of the 30+ Chinese natives I've asked have voted Harvard. One gentleman even asked in disbelief, "You would allow that?" as if the millionaires' club required an Ivy league sheepskin.

These are miniscule sample sizes, I know, but I think they get at something essential. The guy who made his fortune without a strong formal education had to deploy inner resources that are close to the heart for many Americans: hard work, resilience, courage, faith. I also understand that this argument skirts close to de-valuing everything good that comes from a rigorous, formal education. Absolutely not true. I went to college; I want my sons to go to college. Education is important, and when it's done well (more on that in a minute), it's a powerful accelerant for innovation. The problem is, it's not always done right—less and less in the U.S., and all the time everywhere in China. Let me explain.

Schools are inherently conforming mechanisms. They are equally (if not more) interested in making good students as they are in inspiring great thinkers. School is good at telling you what happened; less good at exploring what's possible. School is an important socialization experience, and good at forming a ground-level understanding of the world, but maybe not the best way to get inspired. I think American schools and educators—the best of them, anyway—understand the limits of the institution. They know that for knowledge to deepen as learning requires a non-linear process of acquisition, internalization, examination, and ordering and mastering. It's messy, it's frustrating, and it's entirely individual. Students need a safe space, in the class and in their minds, to be curious and inquisitive. They need encouragement to follow their interests and rewards for experimentation, and even then they fail. Sound familiar? That's the path of invention and innovation too.

High levels of education and economic success don't directly correlate. What nation has the highest level of college grads? Russia, at 54 percent. This is according to a 2010 report from the College Board's Advocacy and Policy Center. Canada, Israel, Japan, and New Zealand follow. The U.S. is sixth with just over 40 percent. Russia is an economic basket case; the others are strong nations to be sure, but not exactly soaring economically. Americans rose so quickly in the global economy precisely because we created an educational system that allowed us to be us—adaptive, inventive, independent.

These qualities are difficult to teach and impossible to test for. Yet that seems to be what American schools are moving toward. And Chinese schools? They're not adaptive, inventive, or independent, but they wrote the book on testing.

It's called the Gao Kao. It's the SAT of China and it drives everything in Chinese schools that happens before it. In fact, the Gao Kao has become not only a measurement of individual performance, but also how schools measure themselves. Chinese high schools are judged based on the proportion of their students admitted to colleges, and no one is admitted without a good Gao Kao. When a high school sends more kids to college, they are rewarded with more funds, a better reputation, and the capacity to attract more students. They are seen as better schools, which allows them to be more selective of the middle school students they accept. Middle schools that place more kids in those high schools get to pick from the best grade school students. You don't have to be a genius to see where this leading: One test means everything, which means everyone teaches the test. This is where some American kid raises a hand and says, "Um, so, what's going to be on the test?"

The Gao Kao tests knowledge in only a few subjects, primarily math, Chinese language, and English, plus some other subjects depending on the province in which one resides. What's more, Communist Party officials have more to say on what's taught and tested than do educators. Talk about a conforming mechanism. Nerve-wracking, too.

Jiang Xueqin is a former principal in Beijing high schools. In *The Diplomat*, he writes:

> *A Chinese school is both a stressful and stale place, forcing students to remember facts in order to excel in tests. Neuroscientists know that stress hampers the ability of the brain to convert experience into memory, and psychologists know that rewarding students solely for test performance leads to stress, cheating, and disinterest in learning. Whatever individual emotions Chinese students try to bring into the classroom, they are quickly stamped out. From the first day of school, students who ask questions are silenced and those who try to exert any individuality are punished. What they learn is irrelevant and de-personalized, abstract and distant, further removing emotion from learning. If any emotion is involved, it's pain. But the pain is so constant and monotonous (scolding teachers, demanding parents, mindless memorization, long hours of sitting in a cramped classroom) that it eventually ceases to be an emotion.*

And you thought your school was tough.

The problem is that American education is moving in exactly this direction. President Bush's *No Child Left Behind* is a school reform program based on "high standards and measurable goals." It requires states to develop assessments and test all students if they want to receive Federal funding. NCLB is reshaping American education, and it's not done yet. In 2010 the U.S. Department of Education released "A Blueprint for Reform: The Reauthorization of Elementary and Secondary Education Act," which advocates for common standards in math and language arts, and a common assessment in all states.

Uh oh.

At the very moment when we need smart, innovative thinkers, we seem to be doing exactly what our rival is doing: making great test takers. But I'm not overly concerned. Education in the U.S. will continue to reflect our own s-DNA better than it mimics another nation's. If there's anything to be concerned about, it what China seems to be realizing. The Gao Kao is undergoing a few reforms of its own: colleges are starting to get more leeway in how (and who) they admit. Keep watching this one; everyone has something to learn.

BELIEF: THE CHINESE ECONOMY IS EXPANDING SO QUICKLY, IT'S JUST A MATTER OF TIME BEFORE THEY OVERTAKE THE U.S.

When China overtook Japan as the world's number two economy, the swoon over China's economic winning streak deepened even further. And people who were already afraid of China just got more scared. So let's look at the GDP figures that are driving the doom and gloom.

Gross Domestic Product is simply a raw accounting of what a nation buys and sells. As typically reported, there's not much finesse in the number, which is part of the problem with China's GDP. The freshest figures for this book peg the Chinese GDP at about $5.3 trillion dollars. What I wish the number said was how much was "demand" and how much was "command."

Innovators, Imitators, and Immigrants

We talked earlier in this chapter about the fundamental difference between a demand economy and a command economy, but some nuance should be worked into the definitions because China is not a pure command economy and the U.S. is not a pure demand economy. The U.S. has done its share of commanding. Military spending is command-driven, same with NASA. The difference is *efficiency*.

U.S. command spending has a way of generating good ideas that the demand economy is ready to run with. The Internet emerged from MILNET, a communication platform first developed to connect the nation's military arsenal. GPS was an Air Force technology long before the public had a chance to buy it. And of course NASA gave us Tang, but also invisible braces, lenses that resist scratching, Temper foam now made famous in Tempurpedic mattresses, ear thermometers, smoke detectors, cordless tools, and water filters. American command spending is more likely to end up producing a product with demand economy appeal. Yes, there's certainly some dumb spending out of Washington that's not going anywhere, but it's not a significant part of GDP activity—much less than 10 percent overall.

In China, command spending is 70 percent of GDP, and most of it isn't in innovative projects; it's in basic infrastructure. That's bad enough, but at least when a major highway is built in the U.S., cars are honking their horns to get on it and go. China's massive highway system has miles of virtually traffic-free sections. Yes, it's all GDP activity, but for what?

Per-capita economic measures tell another story, and this one doesn't require much decoding. China's $5.3 trillion GDP is generated by 1.3 billion people. That's about $4,000 per Chinese citizen. In Japan, 127 million people generated that nation's $5.1 trillion. That's $40,000+ per Japanese citizen. So who's feeling richer, the average first-place Chinese citizen, or the average second-place Japanese citizen? The American economy is roughly $15 trillion per year, by the way. Our 312 million citizens put the U.S. per capita GDP at $48,000 and change. That's real productivity, but not the only measure, either.

Per-person income is yet another way to calm the economic jitters. In the U.S., it's over $24,000, the highest in the world. In China, the average person lives on the equivalent of about $4,000 per year. Closing that gap is what millions and millions of Chinese citizens are now demanding. They are giving their all for the middle-class dreams they were promised. In a very real sense, they are creating economic demand, and testing the limits of what China's demand economy can accommodate.

BELIEF: DEMOGRAPHICS ARE WORKING AGAINST THE U.S.

Let's wrap the chapter on my favorite subject, demographics. Much has been made over the growing imbalance between older Americans and the young workers who will be supporting them, at least economically. In the short term, there are reasons to be concerned. But demographics are a long-view proposition—it's like comparing "weather" to "climate." The short-term data are the evening weather forecast; demographics are the climate, and the American demographic climate is looking pretty pleasant.

Demographers see the U.S. population climbing to 400 million by 2050, while they forecast 1.5 billion in China. By then, only a quarter of Americans will be over sixty years old. In China, it's expected to be 31 percent. But it's the raw numbers that really get your attention: 100 million 60+ Americans versus 456 million 60+ Chinese. In other words, more Chinese people over 60 than there are Americans. That's a nasty forecast, no matter how you spin it.

Apart from age, there's another worrisome demographic fact: the vast differences between China's urban coastal regions and its impoverished rural interior. The 400 million people living in the coastal cities have, on the whole, benefited from the government's economic policies. That leaves 900 million on the outside looking in. One wonders how long "Be patient, we'll get to you" will work, even in the Confucian Chinese society.

Seven

Riding the Continuums: This Way to an American Renaissance

There's a term for Westerners who are enchanted with China's growth and the promise it suggests: Panda Huggers. Not surprisingly, there's a companion term that describes people who are equally bearish: Panda Sluggers. You'd be correct to put me in the second category. After all, the last few chapters haven't pulled many punches on what I (and many others) see just over China's horizon. That said, I don't want to pick a fight.

The economies of the U.S. and China are inexorably linked. At the sovereign debt level, much has been written (okay, shouted) about the Chinese ownership of American debt. I'm not so alarmed. Essentially, the Chinese own about 1.3 trillion dollars in U.S. Treasuries and other U.S. notes. That's about 9 percent of the total. (U.S. citizens and institutions own by far the largest percentage: 42 percent.) There are a lot of zeros in U.S. debt to be sure, but don't let them obscure the equity behind them.

Our debt-to-equity ratio is low and getting lower, and the total U.S. debt is shifting from high-cost personal debt to low-cost government debt. Americans are deleveraging as they age and acquire less, and corporations are flush with cash. In my first book, *Wealth Shift*, this demographic inevitably was center stage. American banks have slowed their lending because huge chunks of the American market don't need the money.

But this chapter isn't about American debt. It's about American assets, and there are many.

MASLOW MEETS S-DNA

Abraham Maslow was the son of Russian immigrants. He was born in Brooklyn, in 1908—a time when the texture of New York City was changing by the boatload. He grew up, got an education, and earned a master's degree in psychology. In 1943, he published *A Theory of Human Motivation,* and gave psychology an entirely new way to understand the human condition. I'm talking, of course about Maslow's Hierarchy of Needs.

Before Maslow and his now-familiar pyramid, psychology was concerned with pathology and abnormality. Before Maslow, it was all Freud and behavior modification—fixing what was broken, in other words. The field of humanistic psychology was born with Maslow's work, which focused on understanding the inner forces that *all* humans share. I've long appreciated Maslow's approach; it's even fair to say this book has a similar ambition. And now that we're here, let's look at Maslow's hierarchy in purely macro-economic terms. As it turns out, he was quite the economic futurist.

The evolution of human economic systems can be understood as continuous progress toward the pyramid's peak, self-actualization. After all, the economy we created at any given point in human history was in service of our needs at that time. On the lowest level, look especially at "food." The first trading systems exchanged tools that helped early humans hunt. It was a crude economy in every sense, but it met the needs. (And I don't mean to offend any

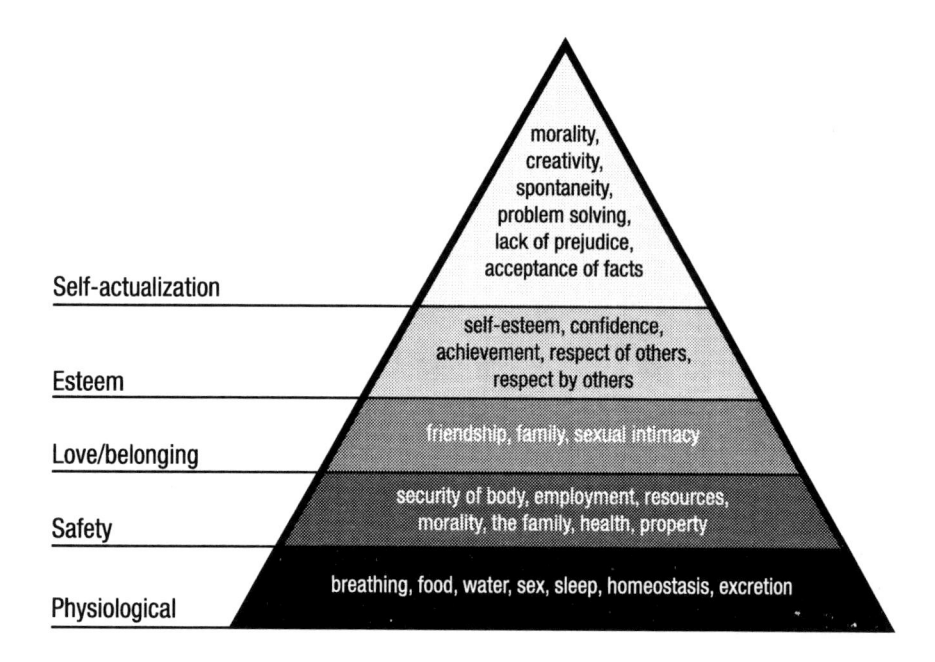

```
                        /\
                       /  \
                      /morality,\
                     / creativity,\
                    / spontaneity, \
                   / problem solving,\
                  /  lack of prejudice,\
Self-actualization/   acceptance of facts\
─────────────────/──────────────────────\
                /  self-esteem, confidence,\
               /  achievement, respect of others,\
    Esteem    /      respect by others        \
─────────────/──────────────────────────────\
            /    friendship, family, sexual intimacy  \
Love/belonging
───────────/────────────────────────────────────\
          /    security of body, employment, resources, \
   Safety/       morality, the family, health, property  \
────────/──────────────────────────────────────────\
       /  breathing, food, water, sex, sleep, homeostasis, excretion \
Physiological
```

delicate sensibilities when reminding readers that at the pyramid's base, the world's "oldest profession" also emerges to meet a basic need—crudely, for sure, but economies aren't inherently virtuous.)

From there, it's a race to the top with everything from ball bearings to iPods arriving to meet the evolving needs of our evolving individuals. The capitalist-based consumer culture thrives in the Self Esteem stage, and for the most part it's where the American economy is located today. You could even argue that this stage is where the Chinese culture—if not the full Chinese economy—resides now. Think about it: Only family is more important in China than earning and maintaining the respect of others.

Let's be clear: There are huge swaths of humanity in China, India, across Africa and elsewhere, where people are locked in the pursuit of safety, economic and otherwise. Self-actualization is out of view when self-preservation is job number one. But people—all people—dream of a better life. The cultural values and economic conditions may give the top of the pyramid a different hue, but everyone hungers to move up.

So what's next for mature economies? Is there a macro-economic manifestation of what seems so wholly individual? Self-actualization, at least in Maslow's vocabulary, doesn't appear to leave much room for economics. Where's the business model in "morality" or "creativity" or "spontaneity"?

I believe—no, I'm certain—that Americans are creating a self-actualized economy, or rather, and economy that enables individual self-actualization. In fact, it's already looking like a growth industry.

What are Facebook and Twitter? At their most essential, these companies help people connect creatively. They provide a platform where problems can be presented and solved. They are tools to help people challenge prejudice and even their own morality. They aren't ideal for any of these tasks, but they aren't finished yet, either. Same with Google, and even Yahoo or LinkedIn. These companies don't make anything, which means they can be about anything. And games? Love them, hate them, or simply don't get them, games are working their way into education, corporate and industrial training, and non-entertainment communications. I heard this the other day: "The nineteenth century expressed itself in the novel, and the twentieth century in film; the twenty-first century will speak through the interface."

All of which the U.S. dominates. Again.

TENACITY 3.0

The United States is in the first years of another global ascent. The first began as the nation itself was born: The Industrial Revolution sprang free from Europe and grew quickly, fueled by abundant American territories and boundless new Americans. In less than a hundred years, the upstart U.S. was punching above its weight class; in 175 years, it had become the heavyweight.

With the development of the transistor and then the integrated circuit in the mid-1950s, the modern computer industry was booted on. The Apollo astronauts carried slide rules on five missions, including the first moon landing, but NASA was among the first to embrace mainframes as a productivity accelerant. IBM built the machines and trained a generation of post-war programmers long before "computer science" showed up on college course offerings. Intel shrank the components and Japan seized the moment. The consumer electronics race was on; the U.S. and Japan became economic frenemies—we needed each other, and we competed fiercely. By the last decade of the century, Japan's role had solidified as the predictable perfectionists of the global economy, while the U.S. propelled the high-tech globalization that has yet to crest.

Today, Apple is one of America's most valuable companies, and the poster company for a high-functioning relationship with China. Apple designs their products in the U.S., has Chinese companies like Foxconn assemble them, then sells them to the world from multiple distribution points around the globe. The work that defines their brand—the product design, the user interface, and perhaps most importantly, the services that make the products so essential—is all done in the U.S. Same with their marketing and sales functions: the best thinkers and the highest salaries reside here.

American companies like Google, LinkedIn, and Facebook and more now model a new kind of capitalist success that's less exposed (if at all) to manufacturing's inherent volatility. They're leveraging the best of American ingenuity and creating entirely new platforms for success for individuals and companies. And are you ready for some delicious irony? Look at how "individualist" America has defined an entirely new model of communal engagement. Through technology we are returning to a state of being where stuff matters less and connections and experiences matter more.

In a way, we're fulfilling our American destiny. The Declaration of Independence didn't claim we had rights to "life, liberty, and the pursuit of increased productivity." No. It said we have the right to go find our own *happiness*. I'm thinking Mr. Maslow heard that loud and clear.

FUNDAMENTALS FOR A NEW CENTURY

The dot-com mania that shaped the Internet's adolescence was infamous for its arrogant flaunting of business fundamentals. For a few short years, "proof of concept" was more important than actual earnings. It was stupid and costly, and the smart people on Wall Street couldn't wait to scold us on our naïveté. At the same time, everyone must understand that a bunch of gamblers on the exchange floor and trading networks are not exactly the best judges of company value. Guess what? It's getting even harder.

I can't paint a detailed picture of where investors should point their dollars. But I can draw the lines that start to give the image some definition, and the first line on the new page is going to trace the most important person in global business: the customer.

We are enveloped by choice, as consumers, as business people with budgets, and as investors. In economic terms, the markets are oversupplied. In oversupplied markets, understanding customers better is what drives company growth. On the other hand, when the markets are undersupplied, operational efficiency is the driver—how well a company gets much-wanted products to the markets. Those companies say: "Here's what we have. Here's how we'll get it to you." That's *talking*. In over-served markets the most important thing is *listening*. Listening to customers, certainly. Every company does market research—some better than others—but listening to customers is a mature part of business. What I'm talking about is listening to *networks*.

Customers talking to other customers is overtaking every other form of market communication. Not just consumer brands and services, either. If you're a procurement officer for a Fortune

500 company, independent thought leaders, consultants, and your peers in other companies have formed an online community where the conversation is lively. It's vital for companies to integrate these conversations into their strategies—to listen courageously, and to join in with grace and humility. This isn't a place for salesmanship or defensiveness. It's a place to reinvent the modern organization around the people who are controlling its destiny. It's hair-raising to be sure, and the models of sustained success are few. But keep watching. The companies that embed this capability into their structures are going to be the companies that propel the United States forward.

BUT…BUT…BUT…

As I'm writing this, America is in a funk.

Actually, just about everyone is. Europe's experiment to scale up their socialist model of statehood as the E.U. is hitting a wall, some of it demographic, some of it just bad navigation. The Arab nations and Mideast are either shaking off despot leaders (a good thing) or paralyzed by what to do now (entirely expected, given their underdeveloped political muscles). Japan is growing old, but their economy simply is growing. India is struggling with massive poverty and food scarcity, an ambitious middle class hungry for more than a chair in a call center, *and* their crazy neighbor with nukes, Pakistan. The Russian economy is dominated by bullies channeling their inner Stalin, all fighting to control the oil because there's just not much else to control. And China, as we've explored at length, is waving to the world from piles of money, but when they look inside there's a poverty of new ideas.

Brazil is a bright spot that's dimmed a bit of late. After a wild ride earlier in the 2000s sent inflation soaring, the Brazilian central bank has managed to slow the overvalued currency by applying the interest rate brakes. Twelve percent will do that. This puts Brazil's

Riding the Continuums 93

cost of credit among the highest in the world. The consumer class that borrowed their way into prosperity is hurting: 22 percent of the nation's personal loans are in default. Maybe the 2014 World Cup and the 2016 Summer Olympics will help, or maybe not.

Back to the U.S., and our funk. The headlines aren't pretty: unemployment up, equities up, then down, then up, then down—it's volatility for volatile times. The politicos are pointing fingers instead of leading the nation, and the citizenry is generally in a foul mood—and with the nation's nose pressed to the morning paper, it's easy to see why. My aim with *Tenacious*, and especially in this final chapter, is to change the view from short term to long term, *real* long term. Thinking in societal demographics broadens the mind, and reveals deeper truths moving underneath the news. And the deep truth within the U.S. should give us all a lot of confidence. The U.S. *will* return to robust growth, and along the way we may just redefine what growth means.

"RECALCULATING"

I love my GPS. She helps me get to where I'm going when I need it, and what I really appreciate is how she gently redirects me when I goof. She doesn't say, "You missed the turn, dork, now you're late and they'll blame me." No. She simply says, "Recalculating." I hear it as, "Whoops, we're a little off course, but I'll steer you right." My point? The current malaise doesn't mean we're dorks; it means we need to recalculate.

American greatness was built on values, not stock indices. We became the nation we are because our immigrant ancestors flourished here. Their ambition was never global hegemony; it was a good life. The current malaise suggests we've gotten too far away from our best selves. A course correction that brings us back to what comes naturally also means that we downshift our consumption. Economic vitality is about more than stuff—that's just consumerism and that hasn't worked; it can't, really, not for a sustained period anyway. The economic strength of our nation should be measured by our ability to use our productive capacity differently, to realign our priorities so that American companies and American innovators (even if they aren't from here) can serve the natural human hungers of a better life. More stuff won't do it. Better ideas will. And the source of those better ideas? There are two; the first is growing in numbers and I hope the second can, too. . . .

PINK SLIPS AND GREEN CARDS

The recession of 2007/2008 saw thousands of Americans leaving their workplaces with their personal belongings in boxes. It's continued with less severity since, and companies have been slow (no, glacial) in hiring them back. For many people, it's been a brutal few years and their fortunes have become the measuring stick of the nation's anemic recovery. It's a discouraging story, but not in the way you might think.

Yes, the profiles of long-term unemployed people are wrenching. But what disturbs me most is that they are profiling the *wrong* people.

Each year, the Kauffman Foundation publishes an Index of Entrepreneurial Activity. It's a respected indicator of new business creation, and they've observed a torrent of new businesses created—the pace of new-business creation in 2009 was the highest since the index began in 1996. In fact, the number of new businesses created during the 2007-2009 recession years increased steadily from year to year. In 2009, the 340 out of 100,000 adults who started businesses each month represent a 4 percent increase over 2008, or 27,000 more starts per month than in 2008 and 60,000 more starts per month than in 2007.

The demographics behind the data are equally telling. Entrepreneurship growth was highest among 35- to 44-year-olds, and the oldest age group in the study (55-64 years) were the second most frequent entrepreneurs. These aren't exactly Mark Zuckerburg types leaving Harvard to change the world; they're older—old, even. Were they carefully plotting for decades to launch their start-ups? My hunch is these are mostly accidental entrepreneurs—experienced and savvy professionals who saw fewer options to earn a paycheck, so they had no choice but to win customers and clients instead. They're too proud and too ambitious to go on the dole, such as it is. So they're doing what Americans do: bootstrapping their way to a better life. Their timing could be ideal.

Recessions are strategic opportunities in disguise. For starters, the cost of doing business is lower during a downturn, especially labor, materials, and office space. The competitive environment is changed as established companies cling to familiar practices and markets instead of venturing into new ones. Or, they enter new markets and new businesses with an increasing desperation. Tough times force entrepreneurs to sharpen their business models faster, helping them to reach profitability sooner. They become companies that are positioned to accelerate when the opportunities increase.

I don't mean to idealize the entrepreneur. Many of these—most of them, actually will fail in the first five years. But some won't, and those businesses will grow, hire, grow more, and become the mid-market businesses that employ the most Americans and create the most wealth. It's happening now, just as it happened during and following every major (and minor) U.S. economic upheaval, including the Great Depression.

Publix opened their first grocery store during the Depression. The Yellow Pages were born to help tapped-out Americans find the best deals without burning gas. Ocean Spray cranberry juice is the product of several cranberry companies that realized nobody was buying cranberry sauce for fancy dinners anymore. Snickers, Tootsie Pops, and 3 Musketeers all launched during the darkest days of the Great Depression, between 1930 and 1932. The list goes on and on, and the reasons then are the same now: Hardship creates opportunities and opportunities ignite imaginations.

Again, accidental entrepreneurs aren't going to change the course of a gloomy nation in a business cycle or three. They are long-term plays, and the new businesses, and business models, of the recession will be a group to watch. They are also the private companies that I believe are going to make some of the best investment targets in the coming decade.

Now, the green card side of the good news. I love the narrative behind this next set of data; it's America's immigration story, refreshed for today's challenges.

A recent study by Duke University, University of California Berkeley, and Harvard University found that almost 52 percent of Silicon Valley startups launched from 1995 to 2005 were founded by immigrants. A quarter of the patents filed during the same period came from immigrants. And research by the National Venture Capital Association shows that 40 percent of the publicly traded, venture-backed companies in high-tech manufacturing today were started by foreign-born entrepreneurs. Look at that figure again: 40 percent of these complex and promising businesses were started by people in very small pieces of the total population pie.

New York City's Center for an Urban Future reveals that while immigrants total 36 percent of that city's of total population, they make up nearly half of all self-employed workers there. The ratios hold up about the same in nearly every major U.S. city, according to the center.

And if you think immigrants have it easy today, I think you're wrong. Some large corporations seek out minority vendors to bolster the corporate citizenship scores, but have you tried to get a green card, or H-1B Visa? There's nothing easy about it. And regardless of how warmly they're welcomed, immigrants are almost always leaving a home and a family to come here. They have guts, ambition, and a stomach for hard work. Immigrants also possess something only outsiders can: a different perspective that views thorny problems in new ways. We've got thorny problems, plenty of them; I just hope we as a nation can back off the anti-immigrant rhetoric and the policies it spawns. Legal immigrants are innovation multipliers. Period.

AND THEN, THERE'S CHINA

Walt Whitman's famous line on his own complexity goes like this:

Do I contradict myself?
Very well then I contradict myself,
I am immense, I contain multitudes.

The Middle Kingdom has never been so accurately described.
For American investors, American businesses, and America as a whole, getting China right is absolutely vital. We've spent a lot of ink cataloguing the multitude of China's challenges, but far less exploring its opportunities, and they are immense.
As China pivots from exports to domestic consumption, there will be countless opportunities for Western companies. There's a growth industry just for consultants who advise American businesses on how to get in to China. Every U.S.-based multinational is there, and most of them are finding that access to Chinese consumers comes at a steeper than expected cost. Some are being required to establish manufacturing facilities in Chinese factories as a cost of entry before they are allowed to sell anything. Others are being forced into stand-alone joint ventures that mandate Chinese companies will have access to the company's intellectual property. That smells bad, even from here.

The human resource departments in American companies are also getting a look at Chinese s-DNA in action. Loyalty to the boss is much more important that loyalty to the company. So when the boss leaves for another opportunity, his or her entire staff is likely to walk as well. This leaves organizations with gaping holes overnight, bleeding away the momentum and sending the recruiting and training costs through the roof.

But I'm punching again.

Doing business that far away from home will always be complex, be it in China or Chile. Some companies won't have the stomach for it, but some will and they may succeed. Over a billion potential customers have a way of bringing out the best effort from the brightest companies. I wish them luck.

Any way you view it, our fates are intertwined. The U.S. relies on low-cost Chinese manufacturing, and China relies on free-spending American consumers. Now let's play out a few simple scenarios.

Scenario 1: China Falters

Let's go ahead and make it a worst-case scenario. China enters a prolonged recession and their economy contracts 50 percent over the next ten years. What impact does that have on the U.S.? Well, the exports that we'd been working so hard to build would probably fall to the floor, a 90 percent drop in exports, let's say. As of this writing, American exports to China amount to 7 percent of our economy; let's imagine we managed to increase it to 10 percent. If we lose 90 percent of that 10 percent, it's a 9 percent hit. That's big. However, we import a lot more than we export, and those imports are going to get a whole lot cheaper. Labor costs will tumble because people in Chinese factories will work for even less than they do now. The radio that retailed for $10 and cost the manufacturer $5, now retails for $7 and costs $3. Sounds survivable, right?

Scenario 2: The U.S. Contracts

Imagine a 5 percent retreat in our economy. Everybody's hurting some, but imports get hurt the most. The container ships arrive less frequently, and less full. We caught a bad cold; China gets pneumonia.

Macroeconomics makes good hypotheticals, but economies are made by real people making real choices, some rational, some impenetrable. Let's bring it home by defining what I think are the most rational decisions Americans, and American investors, can make now, and in the near future.

STAY TENACIOUS: SEVEN IDEAS TO FIGHT FOR

In the context of everything presented so far in *Tenacious*, let me offer a few ideas to take with you into your next conversation on where to point your investments.

The Opportunistic American

It's pretty late in the book to be reminding readers that "buy low, sell high" is encoded deeply into the capitalist genetic code. But clearly, some people just don't get it. In fact, they often get it backwards. Throughout our history, the United States has managed to get other nations to buy our properties—actual or financial, like debt—at premium prices. We then often buy it back at fire sale prices. In the 1980s, Japan bought outrageously priced real estate in New York, Honolulu, Los Angeles, and other pricey neighborhoods. We bought it back when prices returned to solid ground. They bought high and sold low. In consumer electronics, especially TVs and computers, American manufacturers were sold to foreign companies when the margins fell below 6 percent, which seems to be the threshold at which the opportunist impulse can wait no longer. We're happy to let others toil in high-cost, low-margin sectors while we shift our attention and investments to where the higher margins roam, like software and tech services.

At the same time, there's an unattractive aspect to all this opportunism. We saw it most recently during the mortgage meltdown of 2008. As American buyers were smelling the stink inside mortgage-backed securities, German banks were smelling roses, and waving money. We sold, and now billions in bad debt are weighing down German banks just as the rest of Europe needs them to be at their strongest. Call it gross misrepresentation or slick salesmanship: either way, U.S. banks unloaded a bunch of problems—not all of their problems, of course—but enough to move ahead a whole lot lighter in bad debt.

The moral? Markets aren't moral. Markets are opportunities, and Americans are opportunists.

We're Getting Older...Then, Younger than Everyone Else

Yes, it's true that sixty million retiring Baby Boomers are going to take a lot of productive manpower off the grid. Over the next decade, they will produce less and consume more. And as my first book, *Wealth Shift*, detailed how the boomer's consumption has always dominated the market and defined the opportunities. Yes, aging boomers will stress the U.S. Treasury and the entire health care system, but it won't last long.

In the chart on the next page, take a look at what's behind the boomers. In 2020, there will be an estimated 200 million Americans between 18 and 64 adding their productive power to the U.S. economy, while they are supporting about 160 million. Very encouraging.

What about China? The numbers are staggering. You can see that by 2020, China will have roughly 900 million workers

U.S. population growth projection

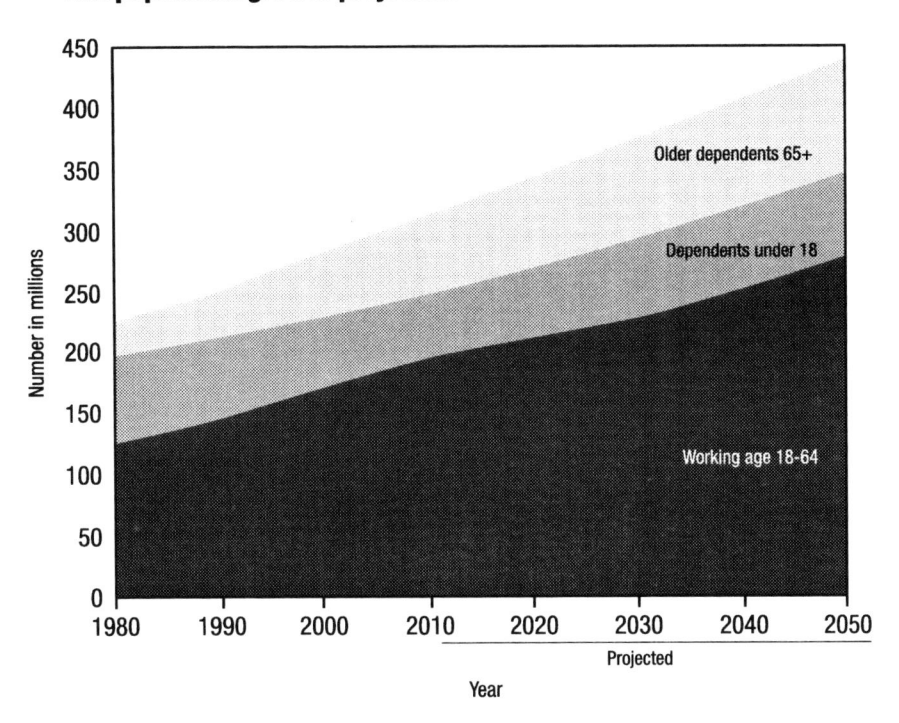

Working age 18-64
Dependents under 18
Older dependents 65+

China population growth projection

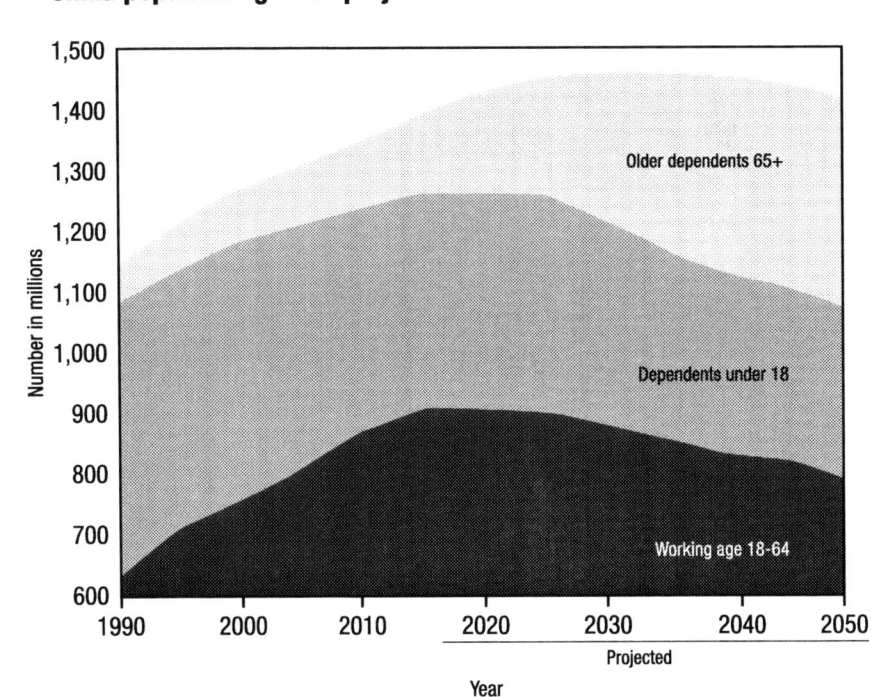

Working age 18-64
Dependents under 18
Older dependents 65+

supporting about 700 million dependents on either side of the age curve. The imbalance looks even worse when you move along the timeline because the productive population has declined significantly more than the dependents, especially the 60+ set. That's trouble.

Dollars Rule, Now and in the Future

I'm not going the take you down the rabbit hole of monetary policy, but you can take it to the bank that the U.S. dollar will remain the world's reserve currency. There are only two other possible contenders, the euro and the yuan. One is failing and the other is a fake.

Europe is broke, or worse, and China won't stop manipulating its currency—the yuan's value has virtually no relationship to China's real economy. That's not uncommon for developing nations, but if the Chinese want their currency to be taken seriously, they need to take off the mask. The valuation screens of currency markets will peg it truthfully, and obviously they don't want that happening. Meanwhile, they keep buying dollars.

China keeps buying U.S. Treasuries because they represent the most liquid and most stable currency available. Even after S&P downgraded the U.S. rating, sales of T-Bills remained brisk; they even accelerated after the downgrade. So much for lack of confidence. And outside of debt markets, the dollar is woven tightly into global commerce. Oil, gold, and other commodities are quoted in dollars. Nearly 90 percent of the trades on foreign exchanges involve U.S. dollars. It's the one currency that allows the world to do business. Not only will it continue, I believe it will strengthen.

Immigration Refreshes Innovative Capacity

There's just no other way to say it: The source of American innovation isn't always American-born. That's our secret formula. And like all secret formulas, from the recipe for Coke to the Google algorithm, it shouldn't be tampered with. Legal immigration should be easier than it is now for educated and skilled professionals. We need to lower the barriers, and confront the naysayers directly with the facts.

When in Doubt, Think Higher Tech

When allocating investment dollars by sector, look for opportunities where radical innovation is possible. This is what the U.S. does better than anyone, especially in software as service platforms. Think mobile, all the time, which is the future of computing worldwide. And keep the viewfinder wider that pure tech companies. Health care innovations—from medical devices to new models of care delivery for aging boomers—can alter entire paradigms. These aren't easy to spot, and they can make you crazy when you do spot them, but I believe there's monster upside here.

Emerging Markets Are Immature Markets

The buzz over emerging markets is becoming so loud that lots of smart people can't hear the voices in the back of their minds. That's the voice of reason, and it's saying, "These places are like America's Wild West—some people got rich; a lot of people got burned." The simple truth is "emerging" means new, as in not mature, as in immature. An immature market is a lot like a teenager: exciting and reckless and impulsive. And talk about drama—you know how the world ends when a teen can't borrow the car? Then an hour later she's in nirvana when that cute boy sends a text? Those kinds of mood swings happen in immature markets too.

China is a twenty-year-old capitalist; the U.S. is 300. It's true there are more early-stage opportunities in China than in the U.S. There's also incredible amounts of risk. Investors can't ignore China, or any emerging market; they also shouldn't load their portfolio with exciting emerging market securities. There's always going to be some teenage drama.

People Don't Change

It's the central idea in the book, and the foundation for every economic prediction I've made here. S-DNA is standing silently behind every decision made by individuals and by markets. And s-DNA simply doesn't change unless it's subject to genocide, prolonged conflict, or massive population shifts via immigration or emigration. China's citizens are the children of Confucius. America's citizens are the children of immigrants.

Governments can command an economy to behave a certain way, at least for a while, but they can't command people to change. True, there are an estimated 90,000 millionaires in China, and lots of media coverage for the superstars of the Chinese economy, but they are vastly outnumbered by the other billion+ Chinese who haven't become capitalists in three generations.

The ongoing disruption in the euro-zone is a timely example. The single currency had a lot of advantages on paper, but the leadership in the European Union apparently failed to account for the wild variations in national characters. Germans aren't French, or Greeks, Spaniards. The money is the same (at least as of this writing) but the s-DNA is not.

A FINAL THOUGHT

As I embarked on *Tenacious* I was more optimistic about China than I became later, as I dug deeper into their economic model. I knew they were smart and industrious people; I wasn't aware of how badly their trust in authority had been betrayed by their leaders. The fate of China will be *the* economic story of the century. They are racing their bike down the twisty capitalist trail; what happens after they wreck—and they will wreck, we all do—will have profound implications on 1.3 billion good people, as well as on the many more trillion dollars and euros jammed into the rider's backpack. We should all wish them luck.

At the same time, we should all reconnect with what has made America the preeminent economic force for nearly a century. Our immigrant-enhanced s-DNA is the sparkplug in the American economy, and by extension, the global economy. That belief didn't change one bit as *Tenacious* came together. If anything, it deepened.

I'm more convinced than ever that the United States has the stuff that successful economies are made of. We have challenges, certainly, some of them immediate and some of them looming. But we've been tested before. Hell, we've fallen flat on our faces before. And every single time, we got back on that bike—a bike we essentially invented and built ourselves—and rode on smarter, stronger, and faster. I can't wait to see where we go next.

About the Author

For more than two decades, Christopher Brooke has been advising high net worth individuals and families, including the executive leaders of several *Fortune 500* companies. In *Tenacious*, he blends his life-long study of economic history with penetrating observations on human nature. His first book, *Wealth Shift*, was published in 2003 and anticipated many of the conditions that are shaping the current global economy.

Acknowledgments

Tenacious is more than this book's title; it's also how it was created. Over the course of developing the book's framework and constructing the manuscript, the global economy and geopolitical environment were in constant and dramatic flux. It took tenacity to look past the news cycle and stay focused on long-term trends.

Once again, I'm grateful for Greg Perry's editorial collaboration. Just as in our first book, *Wealth Shift*, Greg's voice added elegance and immediacy to my demographically based reasoning.

Most of all, I'm grateful for the love, support, and guidance of my wife Marisa who has stood by me though many challenging years, and to our children Tyler B and Tyler D, Brad, Terra and my grandson Dylan. And I will be forever thankful for Denny and Barb Brooke, my parents and my inspiration.